"Jenn is a consummate expert in the field of crave-able dishes and this book is chock full of them. I can randomly open it to any page, make that dish and then feel satisfied from head to toe."

—Lisa Q. Fetterman,
CEO and Founder of Nomiku, and bestselling author of *Sous Vide at Home*

"Jenn's approach to cooking is a source of inspiration; she has the ability to spin comfort food classics and elevate them into something totally new. Additionally, her recipes are easy to follow, and include classic techniques that are simplified for the home cook."

—Molly Adams,
Senior Food Editor of The FeedFeed

"Jenn de la Vega's genuine enthusiasm for making and sharing food is undeniable—if it's all about how you play the game, Jenn is constantly winning."

—Adam J. Kurtz,
Bestselling artist and author of *Pick Me Up*

"If you're interested in throwing your notions of culinary traditions into a blender and picking up some hot tips from competition—and then ending up with something delicious, you'll enjoy."

—Chris Muscarella,
Co-Founder of Field Company

"Jenn is a force in the kitchen. If you are looking to Take Down you̶r̶ ̶r̶i̶v̶a̶l̶ look no further. Jenn's delightful voice, humor and passion for making the most of ̶w̶h̶a̶t̶'̶s̶ ̶o̶n̶ ̶h̶a̶n̶d̶ or tackling that challenging ingredient will guide you expertly to ̶win̶ time again."

"Jenn's unabashed love of food is contagious!"

—Kathryn Tomajan,
Olive Oil Maker and Founder of Eat Retreat

Showdown

COMFORT FOOD, CHILI & BBQ

Bold Flavors from Wild Cooking Contests

Jenn de la Vega

founder of Randwiches

PAGE STREET
PUBLISHING CO.

PAGE STREET
PUBLISHING CO.

First published in 2017 by
Page Street Publishing Co.
27 Congress Street, Suite 105
Salem, MA 01970
www.pagestreetpublishing.com

Distributed by Macmillan, sales in Canada by The Canadian Manda Group.

20   19   18   17   1   2   3   4

ISBN-13: 978-1-62414-376-2
ISBN-10: 1-62414-376-8

Library of Congress Control Number: 2016962395

Cover and book design by Page Street Publishing Co.
Photography by Colin Clark

Printed and bound in the United States

As a member of 1% for the Planet, Page Street Publishing protects our planet by donating to nonprofits like The Trustees, which focuses on local land conservation. Learn more at onepercentfortheplanet.org.

Dedicated to Bernadette
and Jose de la Vega, for staying
hungry and determined.
Hard work and sacrifice have
always been a driving force
in what I do.
Thank you for showing me.

Contents

*denotes award-winning recipe

INTRODUCTION

Hello [Food] World

I'm one of those people who doesn't watch TV anymore or have much spare time. I pack every single moment with the things I love. My philosophy about cooking is very much akin to that of my view of the world. "There isn't a recipe," she says, writing a cookbook. There isn't just one way to do anything, be it a recipe or even your career. I'm always learning and am allowed to be wrong or change my opinion. I hope that when you read this book, you have the ability to experiment with and augment my recipes, find your own way to enjoy them and share it with others. If you have hacks, suggestions for improvement or questions, please do contact me on Twitter: @Randwiches.

My whole life, I've rebelled against traditional paths. Our journey together, here, is no exception. I had busy parents; they cooked for my brother Mark and me when they could and immersed us in Filipino food at parties, but we didn't appreciate it at the time. My earliest taste memories involved day-care scrambled eggs from a box, on an English muffin; burger-chain birthdays; and steamy foil boxes of hot lunch in elementary school. Growing up, finding out where my fast food came from made me not like the idea of cooking. I remember chewing on a piece of chicken nugget and spitting out an errant tendon. I stared at it, puzzled. "Why wasn't it uniform? What was this thing I just had in my mouth?" Quick-service crunchy tacos were my dad's go-to meal when we didn't have time to make dinner. As soon as I found out that the meat was "beef product" and not actual beef on its own, I was done eating it. I also developed an unreasonable fear of hot dogs because I lost my first tooth while biting into one in Mrs. Lee's first-grade class. I was already a picky eater and was eating less variety. No more fast food, but no new, slow food either. I'd later honor these MSG-packed flavors in future recipes, but the difference was conscious transparency in the ingredients I used.

Being around better agriculture and more information made me turn around. The college town of Davis, California, was a good environment in which to learn. The weekly farmers market started as a social obligation but grew into my own form of worship and learning. My food evolution from picky eater to wide-eyed culinary pupil began with a bowl of roasted garlic.

Social functions were a reason for me to look up new recipes and try them out for myself. My best friend, Brian X. Chen, invited me to a potluck. I panicked because I associated that word with large Filipino gatherings, and I'd usually lean on my mother to represent our family. She'd effortlessly turn out a catering pan of pancit glass noodles, rich with pepper and sliced vegetables. I was alone in my college apartment; what could I possibly bring to a potluck? My mom lived six hours away. I did what any newly minted twenty-one-year-old would do—I had a drink. I was at a local wine bar when I was served roasted garlic. I googled how to do it and decided that would be my contribution. I made enough heads of roasted garlic to fill a medium bowl; I picked up a baguette and was on my way to the party. Except, it wasn't a party. It was just two other people. We drank all of the wine and had an amazing night. Along the way, I gradually made my way through the entire bowl of garlic. We didn't believe it; it was so good and so simple. Little did I know the consequences of eating so much allium in one sitting.

My roommates complained of a slight smell emanating from my skin—I became a bowl of garlic. It was so funny that I changed my online chat screen name to "bowl of garlic." What started out as an inside joke soon catapulted me into the world of food.

My food journey is winding and sprinkled with so many stories. A common thread throughout this book is the spirit of competition, creative prompt, personal challenges and difficult tasks. All I know is that I've come out on the other side of it alive! Thank you for joining me.

BASICS

Before we get started, this isn't an ordinary cookbook of winning recipes. In fact, many of them were losers. Therein lies the beauty of innovation! I've taken everything I learned and transformed them into winners. In this chapter, I will expound upon a particular frame of mind, tools and supplies that have helped me throughout my culinary journey.

INTERVIEW WITH MATT TIMMS

"There is something about people wanting to watch competition," says Matt Timms, founder of the Takedowns.

Matt was a self-described dilettante, hosting events in Brooklyn while trying to act, make films and create art. A constant was that he always wanted to have friends over at his house and "be the center of attention."

"I love chili; used to make it all the time," he explained. He redeemed cigarette tabs for a copy of *Marlboro Chili Roundup Flavor It Up: 50 Winning Recipes One Burning Question*—which Matt eventually cooked in its entirety. The appeal of chili is its abundance: when you were low on cash, it could last you a week.

Matt loved chili so much, he joined the International Chili Society (ICS) to judge competitions. He took issue with the strict adjudication and started throwing minicompetitions at home. Later, Matt brought the chili cook-off idea to a trivia night at Bar Matchless in Brooklyn.

"I wanted chili to be 'anything goes,'" he declared. No measuring the cube size of the meat or banning beans. At the Takedowns, Matt focused on amateur cooks for their enthusiasm and range, which reminded him of the camaraderie of the parties he threw. It was about showcasing these cooks in an unpretentious way.

With no-holds-barred, the only element Matt insisted he control was the metal music playing while the audience sampled every chili creation. When the Takedowns expanded to other dishes like mac 'n cheese, salsa and bacon, Matt quit his temp job to run these contests full time around the country.

In fourteen years, Matt has seen six people get married and has hosted events in San Francisco, Austin and Minneapolis. He sums up that the competitors "give such a sh*t," in their cooking and bring heart and soul to the table.

WHAT IS COMPETITION?

I am so unreasonably motivated when people think I can't do something. Even more so when I'm told a food idea doesn't fit into a traditional paradigm of cuisine.

The *Oxford English Dictionary* defines competition in three common ways:

1.   The activity or condition of striving to gain or win something by defeating or establishing superiority over others.

2.   An event or contest in which people take part in order to establish superiority or supremacy in a particular area.

3.   The person or people over whom one is attempting to establish one's supremacy or superiority; the opposition.

The act, event and competitors are all a part of this. Early on in my cooking career, I took losses harder because I was acting alone and had not yet connected with my rivals. Later on when we became friends, we consoled, we commiserated, we lost together. The competitive experience soon became cooperative. Camaraderie is what keeps me coming back, to see what my friends are doing and to catch up.

I'm competitive because I believe in the possibility that I can win. Sure, I could lose, but I think the idea of winning far outweighs the fear of defeat. When I do lose, I am inconsolable for a short period of time. I already know what went wrong and am already calculating in my head how I will do it better next time.

Another definition of competition is the ecological battle for natural resources, like water, food and space. At the root of it all is survival. Many people compete in formal contests or in everyday life to gain an advantage, be it monetary or social. I will admit, I've been lured by the glory of winning. Having my photo on the Internet with a giant trophy feels pretty good. Prizes like free knives, pans and a year's supply of bacon are great, but the outcome was far more impactful on my life's path. For me, the knowledge of how to be successful was an advantage. The repetition of entering and preparing for these culinary bouts gives me structure. I didn't know what I wanted out of a food career when I started to compete in the Takedowns and other local cook-offs. Losing drove me to hone my skills and refine my recipes.

Winning has its own challenges. What exactly does one do with a year's supply of bacon? How can you top your last winning dish?

You don't have to enter cook-offs to innovate and experience the rush of excitement. Ultimately, I think a little contest between friends is healthy. What new foods are we going to experience? How will our experiments move our ideas of food forward?

PERSONAL CHALLENGES

Late one night in my Greenpoint apartment, Matt Kiser said to me, "You know, you could do this."

I was puzzled. "Do what?"

"This grilled-cheese thing! It could be a zine, a food cart and . . ." he went on. I zoned out on the rest of it because up until that point I never considered an actual cooking career. We were cleaning up the empty beer bottles and plates from my latest grilled-cheese night. I was working at a small music promotion company and moonlighting as a TV researcher. My Sunday night grilled-cheese parties were a relief from the New York hustle, a time for my friends from both worlds to get together and veg out. I hated serving and eating the same sandwich twice. Every Sunday for two years, I cranked out odd and interesting interpretations of grilled cheese.

Some of my creations were queso de mano and pico de gallo toasts, Wenslydale and cranberry, as well as truffled robiola and chive. As time went on, I needed to learn about more cheeses. I applied to be a cave intern at Murray's Cheese Shop and began reading *The Cheese Primer* by Steve Jenkins. Matt's comment was a push in the right direction, and I quit my office jobs later that year.

After I finished reading about cheese, I had my nose stuck in *The Escoffier Cookbook: A Guide to the Fine Art of Cookery* for two years to keep my mind harnessed to cooking techniques. Along the way I started blogging. It came naturally to chronicle my food adventures in this manner ever since Mr. Hill assigned "the sandwich project" in seventh grade. We were tasked to write out explicit instructions on how to make a sandwich, from which face to apply the mayo, to its physical assemblage. If you succeeded, Mr. Hill would have to eat the sandwich, if not, you had to eat it. Many of my cohorts failed and attempted to spike their recipes with "gross" combinations like anchovy and peanut butter (strangely enough, together in a winning recipe, Whose Bacon? Nacho Bacon! [page 68] in this book). To be safe, I went for a simple ham sandwich with mayo, lettuce and tomato. I even made him smooth out the air pocket in the plastic baggie so that the sandwich would last until lunch hour. Little did he know how significant this skill became for me.

I scoured Craigslist for cooking jobs. I lacked enough experience on paper or was too afraid to apply. There was just one listing that didn't request a resume or photo. (*Ew.*) It simply asked, "Please send us a paragraph on why you'd like to work at a wine bar in Red Hook, Brooklyn." Cracking my knuckles, I quickly responded with my lack of experience but need for structure to support all of my reading at home and cheese internship.

Honestly, I was shocked I got a response.

Walking in to Tini Wine Bar was a dream. The walls matched the dress I was wearing. I brought a wheel of Mt. Tam cheese from Cowgirl Creamery in San Francisco, not knowing that Monica Byrne and Leisah Swenson were from San Francisco. I trailed Monica in the kitchen for two weeks before she left me alone for dinner service.

I stayed with my "Moms" for a couple years as they expanded the restaurant, renamed it Home/Made and moved it down the street. We catered weddings with me in the kitchen, Monica arranging the flowers and Leisah orchestrating the layout. I remember overhearing one catering consult, "Oh! Jenn's Filipino; she can make lumpia." I poked my head out and stared as if beaming the message, "What?! No I can't . . ." We did our research and pulled off a Filipino wedding menu for 150 people. Even the father of the bride visited me in the kitchen to thank me. It was one of those moments that made all the panic worth it.

I like to challenge myself. Even now, working in an office enviornment at Flipboard, I revel in cooking limitations. Can I make a gourmet lunch for myself with just a microwave? I'm not competing with anyone but myself in these situations. Personal challenges jumpstart my brain, help me keep my skills in check and push me to learn something new.

ABOUT THE RECIPES

We don't talk about failure enough. All of the advice in this book is lessons I've learned from attempting to fry grit cakes on-site at an outdoor venue with no running water or transporting gallons of chili in a New York City cab. The portions were originally made for large crowds and for competition. I've scaled them down for your convenience and to enjoy at home.

You will also find the extremes of meat heaven and restrictive veganism. For a couple of years, I would deliver random sandwiches to hungry worker bees all over New York City. My Randwiches project had no menu and was a creative exercise in catering to a variety of diets, palates and allergies. I got to explore my city and meet many lovely people who love sandwiches. Some of my best ideas are in this collection.

Before you get started, here is some advice for how to use this book.

1. Read the recipes all the way through before shopping or beginning to cook.

2. Vegetables are to be washed in cold water before cutting. Herbs are unbundled and soaked in at least two changes of water to remove sand or grit. Mushrooms should be cleaned with a dry brush or paper towel.

3. Assume that I'm using kosher salt, unless otherwise noted.

4. Dry beans are to be soaked and drained. That liquid is not accounted for in the final recipe.

5. Mincing is chopping finely with a knife. Grating is with a cheese grater. Microplaning is super fine grating.

6. Sautéing and browning assume that you are stirring the food every couple of minutes to prevent sticking, unless otherwise noted.

7. Whisking requires quick incorporation. Folding is more delicate; you must run a spatula around the edges of a mix and then lift from underneath.

8. Anything to do with pickles requires sanitized jars. Steam glass jars and metal lids for two minutes or dip them in a hot water bath before using.

9. Roux is a French paste for thickening sauces. In the case that you do not have flour or butter, a mix of 1:2 cornstarch and cold water will also work.

10. My food processor holds five cups (1.2 L). Consider that if you have a smaller one! You will need to blend multiple batches.

I develop recipes as a remix of something that I know already. Always start with the ingredients and all of the different ways you can prepare them. Once you know the methods, compare all of the flavors that could go with it as well as benefit from the same type of cooking. Explore the overlaps.

What I want to teach you is that you don't just make a recipe and then be done with it. Use what you've learned to apply it and combine with other dishes.

Bring it to a Boil

My roommate Steven Valentino encouraged me to enter an amateur cook-off called the Chili Takedown in 2007. It was hosted by Matt Timms at the now closed Mo Pitkins in the Lower East Side. There were no prerequisites except a fifteen dollar entry fee. I puffed up my chest and was confident my mole chili was going to knock everyone's socks off.

I vividly remember panicking that my stockpot didn't have a lid while calling a car service to drive me and my friend Yan Yan from Greenpoint. Fifteen cocktail tables were arranged in a half circle with foil trays and Sterno cans. We observed the scene as other teams unpacked their streaming concoctions. There was Ida, who always had Star Trek–themed dishes, and Tony Santoro, who I later learned worked on lighting for Sesame Street. When the doors opened, a horde entered, grabbing our small plastic cups of chili samples. I was getting nervous because my Sternos were not hot enough to reduce my very thin looking chili. After the event ended, Yan consoled me as I stirred the leftovers sadly. Everyone else's trays were empty. Matt Timms knew it was my first time, and he encouraged me to try again.

I totally did.

LESSONS LEARNED

- My first chili was very thin. Doubling a known recipe does not always mean doubling the volume and flavor.

- Consider your containers when transporting liquids. Make sure they have lids! If they are hot, you'll need insulation, like dish towels, and the right tools to serve.

- The sting of losing my first contest was even stronger when I realized how much money I spent on ingredients. Budget and track expenses. Even if you win a cash prize, it may not feel like it if you spent too much on fancy ingredients.

HOLY MOLE! STEAK CHILI

MAKES: 4 servings
TOTAL TIME:
5 hours, 30 minutes

I'm really not sure where I got the confidence to enter a chili cook-off. I'd never even made a chili from scratch. Most had been glammed up from a can. In my head it wasn't impossible, and that was an excellent (maybe dangerous) place to start.

What would win? It was a great question, but perhaps I had not done enough research to know the right answers. At the time, steak was the answer. Who doesn't love a steak? Well, in chili situations, I learned the hard way that steak should be cooked quickly or forever. Here is an adjusted recipe for my very first competition chili. The marinated steak is an umami bomb on top of hearty, tomato-y chili.

1 lb (0.5 kg) skirt steak

1 tbsp (15 ml) soy sauce

1 lemon, juiced and zested

2 cloves garlic, grated and divided

2 tbsp (30 ml) olive oil, divided

CHILI

¼ cup (40 g) fresh cilantro

2 tbsp (22 g) sesame seeds

1 medium onion, diced

1 (14-oz [415-ml]) can whole peeled tomatoes

1 jalapeño, seeded and diced

2 chipotle peppers in adobo sauce from a can, chopped

1 quart (950 ml) beef broth

1 tbsp (10 g) corn meal

1 tbsp (7 g) cocoa powder

1 (16-oz [475-ml]) can cooked pinto beans

1 tsp (5 g) salt, plus more

½ cup (120 ml) sour cream

Marinate the steak in the soy sauce, lemon juice and zest, and half of the garlic and half of the olive oil for at least 4 hours or up to 24 in the refrigerator. Remove from the fridge 30 minutes before cooking.

After washing the cilantro, cut off the dirty root ends and discard any discolored leaves. Chop the stems like they are chives and keep the leaves whole. Set aside.

Toast the sesame seeds in a dry pot on medium heat for 2 minutes. Once they release their oils and become a light brown color, add the onion with the other tablespoon (15 ml) of olive oil. Sauté for 3 to 4 minutes. Once they are browned, add the tomato, the rest of the garlic, jalapeño and chipotles. Bring to a boil and reduce to a simmer on medium-low heat for 30 minutes. Break the tomatoes up with a wooden spoon. When the tomatoes have reached a dark red hue, stir in the beef broth. Continue to simmer for another 30 minutes. Add the cornmeal and cocoa powder.

Rinse the pinto beans in cold water and drain, make sure none of the slimy can liquid sticks to them. Fold the beans into the chili with a teaspoon (5 g) of salt, place a cover on the pot and reduce the heat to low. If the mix is still bubbling, move the pot halfway off the heat.

Prepare a grill pan or cast iron skillet on high heat for 10 minutes. Cook the skirt steak on each side for 4 minutes or until a thermometer reads 145°F (63°C) for medium doneness. When I flip steaks, I like to pour in the marinade for extra drama. Once done, let the steak rest on a cool plate or pan with high sides. You don't want to lose all of that precious juice.

When the chili is ready to go, taste it and salt as desired. Stir in the cilantro stems before serving. Garnish each bowl with sliced steak, cilantro leaves and a dollop of sour cream. Congratulate yourself, because this is just the beginning of your chili adventure.

GERI HALLIWELL, YOU KNOW, GINGER SPICE! CHILI

MAKES:
4 bowls of chili
TOTAL TIME:
1 hour

For the next Chili Takedown, I wanted to use an atypical protein. Not ground beef, not steak or bacon. I thought back to my breakfasts at Grandma Lita's house and cutting into these squat sausages called *longaniza*. Puzzled as to what else I could add to this, I took a walk around my neighborhood in Bedford Stuyvesant. I went from bodega to bodega, eyeing the local ingredients. I picked up a six-pack of ginger beer (mostly for myself) and little Jamaica peppers, which were surprisingly hot. I later learned these are known as Scotch Bonnets. As I was starting this endeavor, I curiously poured some ginger beer into the mix and it worked. Ah, more ginger! I ran out and got a hand's worth of the knobby brown aromatic. I ended up with a tangy and sweet ginger broth, topped with a Jamaica salsa verde.

Olive oil

1 medium red onion, peeled and chopped

4 Jamaica or Scotch Bonnet peppers, seeded and chopped

1 lb (0.5 kg) Longaniza (page 58), sliced

1 thumb ginger, peeled and grated

1 clove garlic, grated

1 tbsp (7 g) all-purpose flour

1 (12-oz [350-ml]) bottle ginger beer

1 (14-oz [415-ml]) can whole peeled tomatoes

1 pint (475 ml) chicken broth

1 (16-oz [475-ml]) can kidney beans

Salt and pepper

SALSA VERDE

4 medium tomatillos, husks removed

2 Jamaica or Scotch Bonnet peppers

1 small white onion, peeled

1 thumb ginger, sliced

1 clove garlic

1 cup (240 ml) vegetable broth

1 tsp (5 ml) honey

Sauté the onion on medium-heat with a swig of olive oil until translucent for 3 minutes. Add the peppers, longaniza, ginger and garlic. Cook for another 2 minutes. Add the flour and toss to coat the vegetables. Bring the heat up to high and stir in the ginger beer, tomatoes and chicken broth. Once boiling, reduce to simmer on medium heat. Cook for 30 minutes, stirring occasionally.

For the Jamaica salsa verde, grill the tomatillos either on a grill outside or, like in my early days, straight on the stove burner. Use tongs to flip them as they blister black. Remove the stem and place in a food processor with the peppers, onion, ginger and garlic. Blend until smooth. Cook the tomatillo mix on medium for 10 minutes in a saucepan until it becomes a paste with no residual liquid when you tilt the pan. At that moment, add the vegetable broth and simmer for 5 minutes. Turn off the heat and whisk in the honey. Let cool and store in the fridge until serving.

Meanwhile, rinse the kidney beans and fold into the chili. Cover and cook on low heat for 15 minutes. Add salt and pepper to your liking. Garnish each bowl with a drizzle of salsa verde.

I think this was the recipe that taught me to clean my kitchen as I went along . . .

COCOA CORIANDER CHILI

MAKES: 6 hearty bowls
of chili
TOTAL TIME:
Up to 1 day

This mole-inspired chili incorporates the James Beard burger technique of adding heavy cream to ground beef. Each bite of beef has a mellow note of ancho pepper, while Jamaica peppers provide more of a spicy bite in the broth. It is smoky, creamy and—most importantly—chocolatey.

16 oz (450 g) dry red beans

1 cup (240 ml) water

1 dry ancho pepper

1 lb (0.5 kg) ground beef

2 tbsp (30 ml) heavy cream

Olive oil

1 large yellow onion, chopped

1 clove garlic, grated

⅛ cup (15 g) cocoa powder

½ tbsp (5 g) coriander seeds, toasted and crushed

1 tbsp (10 g) masa harina

Salt

1 bay leaf

1 smoked ham hock

4 plum tomatoes, chopped

2 small Jamaica or Scotch Bonnet peppers, chopped

½ tsp cumin powder

1 quart (950 ml) beef broth

¼ cup (60 ml) plain yogurt

1 bar dark chocolate

Pepper

Wash the red beans, cover with cold water and soak overnight.

Boil the water and soak the ancho pepper for 20 minutes in it until it is soft. Remove the stem and mince the pepper. Fold the pepper into the ground beef and heavy cream. Cover and refrigerate for 4 hours or overnight.

The next day, drain the beans and set aside.

Sauté the yellow onion for 3 minutes on medium heat with a swirl of olive oil, until it is translucent. Add the ground beef and break it up as it cooks. Once the beef is browned, add the garlic, cocoa, coriander, masa harina, salt and bay leaf. Stir to combine.

Turn the heat up to high. Add the beans, ham hock, tomato, Jamaica peppers, cumin and beef broth. Bring the chili to a boil and lower to a simmer. Cover and cook for 1½ to 2 hours. It is done when the beans are tender (not chalky). Add salt to taste.

Garnish with a dollop of yogurt and grate chocolate over every bowl with a microplane.

DIRTY SOUTH BISCUITS 'N GRAVY CHILI

MAKES: **8 servings**
TOTAL TIME:
10 hours

It was during the height of the Paula Deen controversy that Emily Hanhan and I decided to team up for the Chili Takedown. In tribute, we lovingly called her our "horsewoman of the apocalypse" and thought about the tenets of a great Paula Deen dish. We immediately came up with butter and biscuits. What's better than biscuits and gravy? The challenge here was to create a stark white chili with unique flavor and a kick. Enter Advieh, a Persian and ancient Mesopotamian mix consisting of warm spices and rose petals.

1 lb (0.5 kg) dry white beans

2 quarts (1.8 L) chicken broth

1 medium white onion, divided

2 jalapeños, chopped, divided

1 poblano pepper, chopped, divided

1 serrano pepper, minced, divided

6 cloves garlic, minced, divided

1 lb (0.5 kg) ground pork

1 cup + 2 tbsp (240 ml + 30 ml) heavy cream, divided

1 tsp (5 ml) vegetable oil

1 tbsp (7 g) Advieh (page 144)

½ lb (250 g) cooked bacon, chopped and fat reserved

4 tbsp (60 ml) butter

1 tsp (6 g) white pepper

Biscuits, for serving

Wash the white beans in cold water and soak overnight.

Meanwhile, combine the chicken broth with half the amounts of onion, jalapeño, poblano, serrano and garlic. Store in the refrigerator.

Mix the ground pork with 2 tablespoons (30 ml) of heavy cream, the rest of the jalapeño and 1 clove of minced garlic. Store in the refrigerator for at least 4 hours.

The next morning, rinse the beans, drain them and place them in a large pot with the broth. Bring to a boil and lower to a simmer, cook covered for 1½ hours.

Make a sofrito by sautéing the remaining onions, pepper and garlic with the vegetable oil. Careful not to brown the vegetables too much. Cook on medium-low heat until the onions are translucent and the peppers are soft, 5 to 7 minutes.

In another pan, cook the ground pork on medium-low heat, breaking it up as you cook. It should be opaque and no longer pink. Let cool and set aside.

Once the beans are done, blend half of them with an immersion blender or potato masher. Add the meat, Advieh, bacon and sofrito. Cover and cook for 10 minutes. Finish the chili by stirring in the butter, the rest of the heavy cream and white pepper. Enjoy with biscuits brushed with bacon fat.

DIRTY SOUTH POT PIE

What better way to extend a tribute to Paula Deen than with a spin on pot pie? Puff pastry is super flaky and available in most freezer aisles of the grocery store. Using the bacon fat to brush on is not only economical, but gives the crust a salty, savory flavor you don't get from plain butter.

---

2 pieces bacon, chopped

1 small white onion, minced

¼ cup (40 g) carrots, cubed

¼ cup (40 g) peas

2 cups (240 ml) leftover Dirty South Chili (page 25)

1 sheet puff pastry

Pepper

Preheat the oven to 425°F (218°C).

Saute the bacon in a frying pan on medium heat, pour off 1 tablespoon (15 ml) of fat into a ramekin and set aside. Add the white onion to the bacon and continue to cook until softened, about 3 minutes. Throw in the carrots and peas, and cook for another 2 minutes.

In an oven safe dish, transfer the sautéed vegetables. Pour the leftover chili on top. Carefully lay the puff pastry over the chili. Press down on the edges of the pan and cut off any excess pastry dough.

Brush the top of the pastry with melted bacon fat and sprinkle on two or three grinds of fresh pepper. Cut two slashes in the middle of the pie so heat can escape. Bake for 10 minutes, rotate the pan and bake for another 8 to 10 minutes, until the crust is golden brown.

Let the pie rest for 5 minutes out of the oven and dig in, y'all!

ADVIEH BOLOGNESE

MAKES: **Pasta dinner for 2**
TOTAL TIME: **20 minutes**

Whenever you make unique spice mixes or buy specialty ingredients for a single recipe in a book, you're never sure what to do with them. Advieh traditionally goes well with Persian rice, beans and chicken. Here's an unexpected pasta dish using campanile pasta, which is bell shaped, perfect for holding a rich sauce.

1 shallot, chopped

1 tbsp (15 ml) butter

1 lb (0.5 kg) ground beef

1 tbsp (10 g) Advieh (page 144)

1 carrot, chopped

1 cup (240 ml) water

1 (16-oz [475-ml]) can crushed tomato

1 lb (0.5 kg) campanile pasta

Parmesan cheese

Brown the shallot in a pan with the butter for 2 minutes. Add the ground beef and sauté, breaking up the meat with your spoon. Brown the beef for 5 to 8 minutes until it is no longer pink. Add the Advieh, carrot, water and crushed tomato. Cook for 5 minutes on medium heat.

Meanwhile, boil the pasta for 7 minutes until tender or according to the package's directions. Drain.

Toss to combine the pasta and sauce. Finish with grated Parmesan cheese.

THE SMOKEMONSTER

MAKES: 4 (8-oz) portions
TOTAL TIME:
up to 2 days

Fans of the television show *Lost* will know what this is about. For those unfamiliar, it was a science-fiction drama where a plane full of people crash onto a mysterious island. One of the antagonists is a black column of smoke that they call the Smokemonster. It picks up victims and slams them around surrounding trees before dragging them off. It's a scary entity because the show's producers sampled its "voice" from the jarring sounds of the New York City subway. I watched this show religiously with a group of my friends, and when Jeff suggested we make a really smoky chili for the Takedown, this is immediately where my mind went.

We employed our own smoky tasso ham to play the main part here.

1 (16-oz [448-g]) pack dry Roman beans

1 medium onion, peeled

2 jalapeños, stemmed

2 lb (900 g) Homemade Tasso (page 79), cubed

2 tbsp (23 g) brown sugar

1 quart (947 ml) water

1 chile de arbol

1 guajillo pepper

1 (12-oz [350-ml]) jar pepperoncini rings

1 (12-oz [350-ml]) can peeled San Marzano tomatoes

Salt

Soak the beans in a bowl of water overnight, leaving an inch (25 mm) of water to spare over its surface.

Meanwhile, dice the onion and chop the jalapeños into rings. Broil on high for 5 minutes or until the edges char. Set aside.

Toss the tasso with the brown sugar and broil on high for 5 minutes until the sugar melts and bubbles. Let it cool before storing in an airtight container in the refrigerator.

Boil the water and turn off the stove. Soak the chile de arbol and guajillo in it until they become soft. Remove the stems. Using a cup (240 ml) of the soaking liquid, pulse the peppers with the charred onion and jalapeño in the food processor. If it sticks to the sides, add more of the water. Once you've got a mix resembling a watery pico de gallo, combine with the rest of the warm water from before. Set aside until the beans are done soaking.

Once the beans have been constituted, wash them before putting them in the slow cooker. They should appear larger and may have wrinkled skins. Combine the beans with the whole jar of pepperoncini (even the juice!), tomatoes and liquid pepper mix in the slow cooker. Cook for 6 to 8 hours until the beans are tender and not mealy.

Fold in the broiled tasso 30 minutes before you plan to serve the chili. Season with kosher salt to taste.

Additionally, you can prepare the chili ahead of time and let it rest in the fridge overnight to mature the flavors.

2ND PLACE, PEOPLE'S CHOICE 2014 BROOKLYN CHILI TAKEDOWN

LEFTOVER CHILI CASSEROLE

MAKES: approximately
8 servings
TOTAL TIME: 45 minutes

If I had known baking would be this glorious, maybe I'd have given it more of a chance when I was younger. Simply put any leftover chili in an ovenproof pan and top with a batch of cornbread batter.

Suddenly, you have a cozy and filling dinner with little prep. The sweetness of the honey and corn tame the fires of your spiciest chili.

2 cups (475 ml) leftover chili

6 tbsp (90 ml) butter, melted, divided

1 cup (150 g) cornmeal

½ cup (60 g) all-purpose flour

2 tsp (11 g) baking powder

½ tsp baking soda

1 tsp (6 g) salt

1 cup (240 ml) buttermilk

1 egg, lightly beaten

⅛ cup (30 ml) honey

½ cup (75 g) cooked corn kernels

Optional: half a jalapeño, chopped

Preheat the oven to 375°F (191°C).

Place the leftover chili in an ovenproof pan. Spread it evenly and pour 1 tablespoon (15 ml) of the melted butter on top of the chili. Tilt to coat the surface.

Mix all of the dry ingredients together in a bowl. Whisk in the buttermilk, egg, honey and the rest of the butter. Fold in the corn and jalapeño (if you dare!). Pour the batter onto the chili, spreading it evenly with a spatula.

Bake for 25 to 30 minutes or until fork comes out clean when piercing the center. Let cool for 5 minutes, and encourage dinner guests to dig down for a scoop of both chili and cornbread.

LAZY FRENCH ONION SOUP

MAKES: 4 servings
TOTAL TIME:
6 hours, 20 minutes

One time I needed lots of slow-cooked onions for a hot dog topping. A surprising by-product was the cooking-liquid left over. What I didn't was realize how much water they let out. Gosh, it was a lazy way of making French onion soup! Transport yourself to France with this simple soup that packs a punch with caramelized onion and decadent cheese. The recommended cheese can be replaced by any Swiss melting cheese like Gruyère, Raclette or Emmentaler.

To make this vegetarian, replace the beef with vegetable broth.

4 large onions, peeled and sliced into rings

8 tbsp (115 g) butter

1 sprig thyme

1 tsp (6 g) salt

2 cups (475 ml) beef broth

4 baguette slices

4 thick slices cheese, such as Pleasant Ridge Reserve

Place the onions in a slow cooker, making sure to break the rings out individually. Cover and cook for 4 hours, until the onions have released all of their liquid and start to break down. Add the butter, thyme, salt and broth. Cover and cook for another 2 hours.

After the onions are caramelized and the broth is thick enough to coat the back of a spoon, turn on the broiler.

Prepare 4 ovenproof ramekins or bowls with a layer of onion soup, a baguette slice and then the cheese. Broil for 5 to 7 minutes, until the cheese bubbles.

If you do not have ovensafe bowls, place the bread and cheese on a baking sheet and broil. Grate some cheese onto the soups before placing the toasts on top.

BLACK BEAN SOUP

MAKES: 2 bowls of soup
TOTAL TIME: 10 minutes

What do you do with all of that leftover liquid at the bottom of the cooked black beans? You use it!

This is a smooth, cinnamon-y soup to open any dinner party or an easy dinner if you've been at work all day.

2 cups (475 ml) cooked Cinnamon Black Beans (page 117)

1 quart (950 ml) black bean cooking liquid or vegetable broth

2 tbsp (30 ml) heavy cream

2 tsp (10 ml) salsa

1 tbsp (10 g) cilantro, chopped

Tortilla chips

Blend the black bean cooking liquid with the beans using a food processor, blender or immersion blender. If you don't have enough cooking liquid, add vegetable broth.

Warm in a pot over medium heat; do not boil. Before serving, swirl in the heavy cream. Garnish with chopped cilantro and tortilla chips.

VEGETABLE SCRAP BROTH

A redeeming quality of a harsh New York winter is the added comfort of a good homemade soup. I like dumping a bunch of things into a pot and savoring the results under a blanket fort.

When you're making large batches of food, it's easy to generate lots of waste. A traditional way to reuse vegetable scraps is broth. Broth versus plain water adds "what was missing" to a lot of my dishes. It's like the low bass note in your favorite song that you don't notice until it's absent. This broth is unpredictable because your vegetable scraps change from week to week.

The way I make broth is to keep an ongoing plastic bag of carrot tops, green leek tops, onion peels and the like in the freezer until there is enough to fill the bowl of my slow cooker. When I've reached peak veggie-scrap, I cover it with water and slow cook for at least 4 hours. Vegetable broth doesn't take as long as meat.

Depending on the cuisine of the planned dish, I add different aromatics. At minimum there is always 1 bay leaf and 1 teaspoon (6 g) of whole peppercorn.

For Latin-American flavors, add 1 teaspoon (6 g) cumin seed and 1 teaspoon (6 g) coriander seed.

For "seafood" flavors, add 1 teaspoon (6 g) dill and 1 teaspoon (6 g) fennel seed.

For Chinese flavors, add 1 teaspoon (5 ml) soy sauce and 1 star anise pod.

For French Provencal flavors, add 1 teaspoon (6 g) each of sage, thyme and rosemary.

Once the broth is done, strain and place in plastic quart containers. Let them completely cool. Leave room and label them if you will be freezing them. I prefer to keep broth in pint containers instead of large gallon drums so I can quickly grab quantities without defrosting all of it.

HOT HAM WATER DASHI

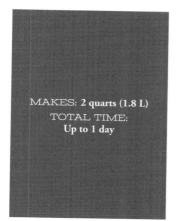

MAKES: 2 quarts (1.8 L)
TOTAL TIME:
Up to 1 day

One year, Jeff got me a smoked ham leg for my birthday. I was thrilled! Consuming the whole thing was a cooking challenge in itself. What I didn't know about it is that you have to peel away the tough, salty and inedible skin. The instructions say to bring the leg to a butcher and ask them to slice it. I'm really stubborn and always say "I CAN DO IT MYSELF." Let me tell you, it's really hard without a machine. Now, I know not everyone will have access to a whole ham leg, but in case you do, I implore you to try this broth. It works with ham rinds, salt pork or bacon, too.

Hot ham water is a reference to one of my favorite shows, *Arrested Development*. When Buster Bluth tries a sip of this dish he says, "It's so watery, and yet, there's a smack of ham to it." (Hopefully more in my version.)

Dashi is the foundation of ramen and can be the liquid you use to cook rice, beans or any other grain.

1 lb (0.5 kg) ham skin

Water to fill a slow cooker

1 handful bonito flakes or 3 chopped anchovies

Place the ham skin in a slow cooker and fill with water. Cook on low for 8 hours or overnight. Discard the ham. Stir in the fish and store in the fridge for 8 to 12 hours. Strain the broth and taste for saltiness. Dilute with as much water as needed to your taste. It might congeal, and that is normal; it will liquefy when heated again.

HOT HAM WATER RAMEN

MAKES: **2 small lunch servings**
TOTAL TIME: **25 minutes**

Traditionally, country ham is cured and smoked. It is so salty, you have to soak it or simmer it in water to dilute. With a whole ham leg at my disposal, I was eating fried ham biscuits with honey butter or grainy mustard for the first week. Heaven forbid my love of biscuits should falter! It was time to shake it up. This was the first iteration of ramen I ate with my hot ham water. You can substitute any vegetables, but the crispy fried ham makes it so delightfully porky and indulgent.

3 cups (710 ml) Hot Ham Water Dashi (page 35)

1 pack ramen noodles

2 eggs

2 garlic chives, chopped

¼ lb (113 g) greens like arugula or cabbage

1 spring onion, whites sliced into rings

1 slice ham, fried and sliced into strips

1 tbsp (10 g) crispy onions

Bring the hot ham water to a boil in a small pot. Add the ramen noodles and cook for 3 minutes or until tender. Remove the noodles to your serving bowls.

Lower the heat to a simmer and carefully poach the egg for 4 minutes, one at a time, in the broth. Remove with a slotted spoon and place on top of the noodles. Ladle the broth into the bowls and garnish with the remaining ingredients.

TONKOTSU BROTH

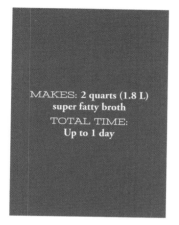

MAKES: 2 quarts (1.8 L)
super fatty broth
TOTAL TIME:
Up to 1 day

One of the most basic principles of cooking is a good broth. Some of the best broths I've had have been at ramen houses where cloudy *tonkotsu* pork reigns. I've been corrected on Twitter because I've been referring to it as *tonkatsu*, which is actually a fried pork cutlet. I also acknowledge that there is no dashi in this recipe. That is because it was meant to supplement a Whose Bacon? Nacho Bacon! (page 68). For a truer ramen experience, add 2 mashed anchovies or 1 cup (26 g) of bonito flakes to the second broth below.

The combination of bacon and chicken rounds out the spiciness of the ginger and garlic over time.

You can either follow my slow cooker method or use a large stock pot. The latter case requires you to watch the broth, skimming crud off the top and making sure the bottom doesn't burn. I had a lot of steps because I went to work during the day, and this was the easiest way to keep the broth going, unwatched.

½ lb (250 g) bacon

1 carrot

1 onion, peeled and halved

2 bay leaves

½ head garlic, peeled

2 fingers worth ginger, peeled

4 scallions

1 Cornish game hen

1 lb (0.5 kg) smoked ham hocks

1 tbsp (10 g) peppercorn

Place the bacon, carrot, onion, bay leaf, garlic, ginger and scallion in the bowl of a slow cooker. Cover with water and cook on low for 8 hours. Carefully remove the vegetables without mashing them. Strain the broth.

Put the chicken in the slow cooker with the broth. Add more water to completely cover. Slow cook for another 8 hours until the meat falls off the bone. Strain the broth and clean the chicken for usable meat (for another recipe!). Save the bones; set them aside.

Add the ham to the slow cooker with the broth. Cook for 4 hours until the meat falls off the bone. Strain again. Pick usable meat off the bones (for Whose Bacon? Nacho Bacon!, page 68). Combine the pork and chicken bones on a baking sheet, broil the bones for 8 to 10 minutes or until they turn a toasty brown color.

Finally, add the peppercorn and roasted bones to the broth in the slow cooker. Cook for 4 hours and strain one more time. Taste it and add salt, if needed. If it's salty, add water.

Let the broth completely cool and store in the fridge. In an hour or two, you will be able to scrape off the layer of opaque bacon fat from the top. Save it for frying or another project.

The broth will be gelatinous but rich. Apply heat, and it will melt down to soup again.

NANAY'S ARROZ CALDO

MAKES: A hearty pot for
4 people to share
TOTAL TIME:
1 hour, 45 minutes

Again, I blindly entered a new competition without any real experience. The Soup Takedown was on the day of the 2015 Super Bowl at Littlefield in Brooklyn. The default soup I knew how to make without a recipe was *arroz caldo*, a Filipino congee. My family generally makes it when you're feeling sick or when you need to get rid of a lot of leftover rice. The dried-out rice, just like fried rice, is perfect for soaking up flavors. In my attempt to update this idea, I developed a chicken dust topping based on the idea of pork sung or sweet pork floss. I was browsing around Chinatown and upon closer speculation, discovered pork floss is basically fluffy jerky.

Say goodbye to sniffles because the lemon and ginger in my version of chicken soup will clear you right up.

---

1 whole chicken

1 bay leaf

1 tsp (6 g) whole peppercorn

¼ cup (60 ml) Asian fish sauce

1 thumb ginger, peeled and grated

1 tsp (6 g) freshly ground pepper

2 cups (300 g) white rice, cooked (preferably day-old)

4 scallions, sliced into rings

1 lemon, juiced

½ cup (30 g) Chicken Dust (page 144)

Boil the chicken whole, in enough water to cover it, with the bay leaf and peppercorn. After 10 minutes, bring down to an aggressive simmer, just so the water isn't popping out of the pot. Be careful to pour in more water as it evaporates to make sure the chicken stays submerged. Try to turn the chicken a few times during cooking and skim off any fat that floats to the top. Cook for 45 minutes until the chicken is fork tender. What does that mean? When you stick a fork into the chicken and pull, it comes off easily and white, not still pink or red. A thermometer should read an internal temperature of 165°F (74°C). Turn off the heat and save the broth you just made.

Preheat the oven to 400°F (204°C). Once the chicken is done, pull it out of the water and put it on a baking sheet. Pull all of the meat off and break the chicken meat into bite-size pieces, toss with the Asian fish sauce. Set aside.

Roast the bones in the oven for 15 minutes or until browned. Place the bones back into the cooking water and simmer down to 1 quart (947 ml) of liquid. Skim off any fat and strain the broth.

Combine the broth, ginger, pepper and rice in a pot. Bring it to a boil, making sure to break up the rice. Simmer for 20 minutes and fold in the chicken. Turn off the heat and let rest for 5 minutes, covered.

Garnish each bowl with scallions, a teaspoon (5 ml) of lemon juice and one spoonful of chicken dust.

The easier version of this dish is to boil it all together, bone-in and all. Put in the work in prep or gnaw it off the bone—tastes great either way!

JUDGE'S
HONORABLE MENTION
2015 BROOKLYN SOUP
TAKEDOWN

Roll With It

Fast forward to 2013. Matt Timms has expanded the Chili Takedown to focus on other types of food on a quarterly basis, and he put out a call for cooks. I threw my hat into the ring with no prior knowledge of how to make meatballs. All of the meatballs I ate growing up were premade, in a microwave TV dinner or from an Italian fast food restaurant. It just wasn't a dish that my family was familiar with cooking.

My roommate Jeff Stockton and I did a lot of research. We consulted books, online recipes and visited the Meatball Shop in Williamsburg. Our favorite sources were Mark Bittman and Alton Brown. We tested meatballs for two weeks and considered the texture, cooking methods and flavor profiles. I marked up a cupcake tin with dry-erase marker to observe the different proportions of spice. This battery of tests was how I got into developing recipes.

Making a great meatball mix is a stepping-stone into making sausage. Meatballs need to bind and stand alone. Encasing the meat adds a whole new, juicy dimension that can be transformed through grilling, braising, smoking and curing. This set of sausage recipes has a very colorful story behind them.

I had promised to do a post-competition sausage pop up at Project Parlor, and I thought, "Sausage is easy to make, right?" My poor roommates, Jeff and Dylan, were baffled by the task, how do we encase the sausages without a stuffer? Someone had a brilliant idea to use a system of cut up two-liter bottles. It took two of us to hold, a panic of tamping meat down with a spoon, all while holding the casing in place. It took way too long! With our collective tails between our legs, we quickly jumped online and bought an attachment for our mixer.

So far, many of the competitions I've been in have been judged on one-bite servings, and meatballs are the perfect portioning size to make a big impression.

LESSONS LEARNED

- Test. Test. Test. When you embark into uncharted waters, you need to budget the time to test.

- It isn't enough to just think your recipe is good. Consult friends, family, roommates or coworkers when taste-testing. You're not just cooking for yourself. Your recipe must appeal to a wide spectrum of palates.

- When scaling up a recipe, add the originally stated amount of salt. Fry a test piece and taste it before adding the rest of the salt. It will likely be less than you think.

- Meatballs are great for parties because you can vary their size depending on their use and bake trays at a time.

FUZZY FIVE-SPICE MEATBALLS

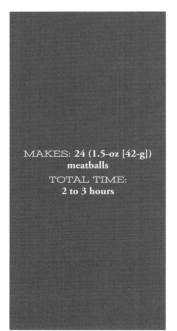

MAKES: 24 (1.5-oz [42-g]) meatballs
TOTAL TIME:
2 to 3 hours

I cleaned up various cuts of meat, and Jeff set up our brand new meat grinder attachment for our mixer. *Nota bene*: always read the instructions before trying new appliances. We failed to cut the meat into long thin strips, so they fed into the grinder funny and got stuck a couple times. Our main foci for meatball development were texture and flavor. Brown's meatball base calls for grinding the meat twice, and Bittman suggests a ½ cup (120 ml) of milk, so we did both!

Once everything was mixed, we divided the mixture into bowls and flavored four types of meatballs. We pan cooked one of each type on all sides until the instant-read thermometer registered an internal temperature of 160°F (74°C). We didn't want no raw meats!

The assembly line for the big finish took a nod from Best Pizza in Williamsburg, who rest their meatballs in bacon fat. Jeff admitted that he felt pretty uneasy about that step, but I insisted that we try it. We took it one step further and rolled the meat in crushed pork rinds for more crunch when you bit into the ball.

Despite losing our first Meatball Takedown, Jeff and I love this recipe. It is a friendly, hearty meal that hits the spot. It is salty and decadent from the bacon, yet warm from the cinnamon infused tomato sauce. An indulgent pork-rind crust is our fatty factor and stems from an old Escoffier tradition of sprinkling breadcrumbs onto poached meats instead of breading and frying. The hit of anchovy at the end is our secret weapon, delivering that pungent umami that sets it apart from your traditional Italian fare.

---

1 (28-oz [840-ml]) can whole roma tomatoes

1 (6-oz [180-ml]) can tomato paste

1 cinnamon stick

1 garlic clove, grated

¼ tsp smudge anchovy paste or 2 whole anchovies, crushed

MEATBALLS

½ cup (120 ml) heavy cream

1 tsp (6 g) salt

½ cup (45 g) Parmesan cheese

2 cloves garlic, grated

1 tsp (6 g) red pepper flake

1½ tsp (8 g) dried basil

1½ tsp (8 g) five-spice powder

1 lb (0.5 kg) ground beef chuck

1 lb (0.5 kg) ground pork shoulder

½ cup (30 g) bread crumbs

½ lb (230 g) bacon

4 oz (112 g) spicy pork rinds

(continued)

FUZZY FIVE-SPICE MEATBALLS (CONT.)

Place a large bowl in the freezer, if it can fit. Alternatively, nest a bowl of ice under a metal bowl.

Put the roma tomatoes in a pot with the tomato paste, cinnamon and garlic. Bring the sauce to a boil, then cover and lower to a simmer for 30 minutes. Remove the cinnamon stick. Crush the tomatoes with a wooden spoon or potato masher and continue to simmer for another 30 minutes.

If big bubbles splatter all over the place, add a ½ cup (120 ml) of water and stir. Cook 15 minutes until the tomato sauce has darkened to a deep red color. When you taste it, it should not be bright, but mellow and sweet.

Add the anchovy and turn off the heat. Let it cool completely before you taste again. You want the aggregate salt from the meatballs and the bacon rind garnish to be balanced. If you think the sauce needs a touch more salt, DON'T DO IT.

In another bowl, mix the heavy cream with the salt, Parmesan, grated garlic, red pepper, basil and five-spice powder in a small bowl.

Using gloved hands, lightly break up the ground meats in your frozen metal bowl. Mix in the bread crumb and spiced liquid. Be careful not to overwork the mix. Try your best to fold and incorporate until the liquid is absorbed. Cover and rest in the refrigerator for 1 to 4 hours.

Cook the bacon on medium heat 3 minutes a side until crisp and pour off the fat and save it for later. Sneak a piece but crumble the rest in the food processor. Place the bacon in a plastic container lined with a paper towel. Next, pulse the pork rinds in the food processor. Mix with the bacon and store until you're ready to serve.

Preheat the oven to 400°F (204°C).

Test and taste a small portion of the meatball mix by frying a sample for 2 minutes on all sides, until the internal temperature of 160°F (71°C). Adjust the seasoning if needed. When you're ready to cook the meatballs, form them with a measuring tablespoon or small ice cream scoop. Be generous with the tablespoon, if you were to level it off, you'd end up with 30+ meatballs. If you have more than 24, just redistribute the meat to make the balls even.

Place them in an ungreased, lined pan and bake for 20 minutes, until the internal temperature reads 160°F (71°C). Turn off the oven and drain the juices from the meatballs. (Save it for a broth later!) Toss the meatballs in the bacon fat and put back in the oven to keep warm.

When you're ready to eat, prepare bowls with a scoop of tomato sauce. With a slotted spoon, roll each meatball in the pork rinds and bacon before placing in a bowl of sauce. Moan.

CROUCHING TIGER, HIDDEN PASTA

MAKES: 25 surprises
TOTAL TIME:
1 hour, 15 minutes

Using the same Fuzzy Five-Spice Meatball (page 42) mix, surprise and delight your guests with a meta-meatball. As the meat mixture rests in the fridge, prepare the tiniest ravioli, ever.

The miso is a tasty compliment to these flavor packed meatballs.

1 egg

48-cm (19-in) square fresh pasta sheet

½ cup (120 ml) Miso Pesto (page 145)

Fuzzy Five-Spice Meatball Mix (page 42)

Whip the egg with a fork in a small bowl.

On a cutting board with food-safe scissors or a large chef knife, cut 24 rectangles of pasta, measuring 1 x 2 cm (0.4 x 0.8 inch).

Using the end of a chopstick, dot one side of pasta with pesto and then add a dot of egg. Fold the rectangle in half and seal.

Divide the meat mixture into 24 evenly sized meatballs. Dig your thumb into each ball to create a divot, place the tiny ravioli inside and pinch the meat around it to close. Roll the meatball between your hands to ensure the pasta isn't poking out the other side.

Once all of the meatballs are formed, let them rest in the fridge for 15 to 30 minutes.

Preheat the oven to 350°F (177°C). Drizzle olive oil over the meatballs and cook for 15 minutes. Raise the oven temperature to 400°F (204°C) and cook for 5 to 10 minutes, until the internal temperature reaches 160°F (71°C). Test a ball to see if the pasta is cooked and the meat inside is not pink.

BLACK BEAN AND PEPITA BALLS

MAKES: 30 (1-oz [28-g])
meatballs
TOTAL TIME:
2 hours

How do you bind seemingly chunky ingredients together in a ball without using eggs, cheese or cream? The answer is *panada*. In some cultures, panada is known as a bread soup. Panada is also a thickener made of soaked bread crumbs in either water, broth or milk. In this case, the liquid released from the cooked vegetables will bind with the bread crumbs and blended beans.

These non-meatballs get their heft from black beans with help from savory shiitake mushrooms and crunchy pepitas.

---

1 large onion, peeled

2 carrots

2 celery stalks

1 garlic clove

½ lb (250 g) shiitake mushrooms, wiped clean and stems removed

¼ cup (40 g) kale

2 tbsp (30 ml) olive oil

2 tsp (11 g) salt

½ tsp cinnamon

2 tbsp (30 ml) tomato paste

2 cups (475 ml) cooked Cinnamon Black Beans (page 117) (or canned is okay, too!), divided

1 tbsp (10 g) fresh oregano or ½ tbsp (5 g) dried

¼ cup (45 g) nutritional yeast

1 tbsp (15 ml) white miso

1 cup (150 g) bread crumbs

½ cup (75 g) pepitas

Place the onion, carrot, celery, garlic, mushrooms and kale in the bowl of a food processor. Pulse a few times to break everything down uniformly as small as pebbles; make sure there are no large chunks.

Start a frying pan on medium heat with the olive oil. Transfer the vegetables to the pan and cook for 10 minutes, stirring occasionally. As the vegetables release water and start to brown, add the salt, cinnamon and tomato paste. Cook for 5 more minutes, remove from the heat and let it cool.

Meanwhile, add half of the black beans, oregano, nutritional yeast, miso and a scoop of the cooked vegetables to the food processor. Pulse to form a paste, scrape down the sides and continue to process. If it is not blending, add any liquid gathering in the pan of vegetables.

Combine the cooked vegetables with the bean paste in a large bowl. Fold in the bread crumbs, remaining black beans and pepitas. Cover and completely cool in the fridge for at least an hour.

Once the mixture is completely cool and you are ready to cook, preheat the oven to 400°F (204°C).

Use cooking spray or a paper towel soaked with olive oil to grease a quarter sheet pan.

With a small ice cream scoop or tablespoon, shape 30 balls. As you make them, press the cup of the scoop against the side of the bowl to pack it well. That way, each ball is consistently the same size.

Drizzle a bit of olive oil over each row of balls and bake for 20 minutes. Check the bottom of the balls for browning and crust forming on their tops. They are not done if they break when you pat the top.

Let the meatballs cool for 5 minutes before serving. I advise you not to hold them in sauce but pour sauce over them, if you must. They will fall apart with tongs, so use a spatula, spoon or dainty fingers.

CHERRY CHOCOLATE MEATBALLS

MAKES: 32 meatballs
TOTAL TIME:
6 hours

The introduction of Amarula, a South African cream liquor, lends a creamy touch that plays well with the warm spices of cinnamon and chocolate. If you can't find Amarula, substitute with amaretto, RumChata or any almond-flavored coffee creamer.

If you don't have a food processor, use ground pork and chop the fat as best as you can.

2 lb (0.9 kg) pork, cubed

½ lb (250 g) pork fatback

¼ cup (60 ml) dried cherries

3 tbsp (45 ml) Amarula

1 tbsp (15 ml) soy sauce

2 tbsp (30 ml) brown sugar

¼ cup (50 g) dried shallots or onion, crushed

2 tbsp (20 g) cocoa powder

2 tsp (11 g) salt

1 tsp (6 g) fennel seed

1 egg

1 tsp (6 g) cornstarch

1 bar dark chocolate

A dash ground cinnamon

Olive oil

½ cup (30 g) crushed buttery crackers

Cube the pieces of pork and fat, removing any hard pieces of skin. Store in the freezer for 30 minutes or up to an hour. Soak the cherries in the Amarula and soy sauce at room temperature during that time.

Meanwhile, combine the rest of the ingredients except the cracker crumbs in another large mixing bowl.

Once the meat is cooled, pass through a meat grinder. If you are using a food processor, work in batches pulsing lightly until the meat is broken down into small pellets. Do not put the whole bowl into the machine or it will get stuck.

Fold the meat into the aromatic mix, cherries and crumbs, careful not to overwork it. Chill the mixture for at least 4 hours.

Preheat the oven to 450°F (232°C).

Scoop 1-ounce (28-g) balls onto an oiled baking sheet and bake for 15 minutes, until it reads an internal temperature of 160°F (71°C).

Transfer the meatballs to a serving dish and finish with a shave of dark chocolate.

GIMME KIBBEH

MAKES: **10 large kibbeh**
TOTAL TIME: **1 hour**

Kibbeh are Middle Eastern fried meatballs studded with wheat, slightly similar to Spanish *albondigas*, which have rice. They're meta! You stuff raw meat with a mix that is cooked and then fry the whole thing.

I stumbled upon an ancient grain called einkorn at the Union Square Farmers Market. It's got a tougher mouthfeel that I like, but if you can't find it, replace it with barley.

Fragrant with allspice, lemony sumac and cumin, these fried meatballs will surely take you to another land.

---

1 cup (150 g) einkorn, cooked and drained

2 tsp (11 g) salt, divided

1 cup (240 ml) Savory Yogurt (page 152)

1 clove garlic, grated

1 lb (0.5 kg) ground lamb

1 shallot, grated

¼ cup (40 g) macadamia nuts, chopped

¼ tsp cayenne

½ tsp cumin seed

1 tsp (6 g) allspice

½ tsp sumac

1 egg, beaten

Vegetable oil

Black pepper

Bring a small pot of water to boil. Add the einkorn and a pinch of salt, bring down to a simmer and cook for 30 minutes until tender. Drain off the water and let cool.

Preheat a Dutch oven with an inch (25 mm) of oil on medium heat, up to 350°F (177°C).

Mix the yogurt with the grated garlic and ½ teaspoon of salt. Set aside.

Knead the rest of the ingredients in a bowl, except the egg and olive oil. Take ⅔ of the meat mix and blend it in a food processor with the egg to form a smooth paste. Sauté the remaining third of the mix with a bit of olive oil in a frying pan for 5 minutes until the lamb is browned and no longer pink.

Wearing plastic gloves, scoop a 1-ounce (28-g) portion of the raw blended paste and flatten it in your hand, fill it with 1 teaspoon (3 g) of the cooked coarse mix and seal it into a ball. Continue to fill balls of paste with the rest of the meat mix.

Fry the kibbeh in 2 inches (5 cm) of vegetable oil for 10 to 12 minutes until browned on all sides. Drain on paper towels and keep warm in a 175°F (80°C) oven.

Serve the kibbeh on a swipe of Savory Yogurt and freshly ground pepper.

20K MEATBALLS UNDER THE SEA

MAKES: 4 full-size sandwiches

TOTAL TIME: 5–10 minutes

We argued about whether this sandwich was a sub, hoagie or grinder. Since we're in Brooklyn, I'll argue for the sub on account of the particular bread you use for hoagies in Pennsylvania. In any case, this is a fan favorite from the Project Parlor series.

Crisp, fatty bacon accompanies my Fuzzy Five-Spice Meatballs (page 42) in an easy to hold bun.

4 sub sandwich rolls

2 tbsp (30 ml) melted butter

4 slices cooked bacon

½ batch Fuzzy Five-Spice Meatballs (page 42) in sauce

Parmesan cheese

Split the sandwich rolls enough that you leave a hinge. Brush their insides with butter and grill them lightly to toast. Or, toast them in the oven for about 5 to 7 minutes.

Fill each roll with a slice or two of bacon, then pile on three meatballs in sauce. Friggin' cover them in freshly grated Parmesan cheese. I'm not talking about powder-can cheese, but Parmegiano Reggiano grated from a block.

MEATBALLIN' TRIBUTE

MAKES: **a large bowl
dinner or one modest shared
plate for two**
TOTAL TIME: **20 minutes**

My favorite dish to order at the Meatball Shop is their spicy pork meatballs over rigatoni and pesto. I'm usually a very peckish eater and never finish my plate, but for some reason, I'm moved to feral voraciousness around these. Miso Pesto will go with pretty much any meatballs in this chapter, as a much appreciated herby kick to balance out the fatty mouthfeel. Here's how I honor this dish at home.

1 lb (0.5 kg) rigatoni pasta

**⅓ cup (80 g) Miso Pesto
(page 145)**

8 meatballs of your choice

Parmesan cheese

Bring a pot of salted water to a boil. Add the rigatoni and cook for 8 minutes until the noodles are opaque and you can bite through them or according to their directions. Reserve 2 tablespoons (30 ml) of the cooking water and then completely drain the pasta. Stir the reserved cooking water with the pesto and toss with the pasta in a bowl. Top with the meatballs and a generous shaving of Parmesan cheese.

CHINESE SAUSAGE

MAKES: 10 (6-inch
[15-cm]) sausage links
TOTAL TIME:
4 hours, 15 minutes

Dried *lapcheong* is notably hard and sweet. I wanted to come up with a soft, fresh sausage version of it. Condensed milk adds a thick, sweet flavor alongside the spicy ginger and mellow note of scallion.

If you do not have a meat grinder or sausage stuffer, you can make patties or uncased "links" to bake or fry before slicing.

5 feet (152 cm) sausage casing

2½ lb (1.2 kg) stew pork, cubed

⅔ lb (300 g) solid fatback, skin removed and cubed

2 tbsp (30 ml) sesame oil

2 tsp (10 ml) rice wine vinegar

4 tbsp (60 ml) condensed milk

1 tsp (6 g) sesame seeds, toasted

2 stalks scallion, chopped into rings

1 inch (25 mm) piece of ginger, peeled and minced

1 tbsp (10 g) granulated sugar

1½ tbsp (30 g) salt

Soak the sausage casing in water. Change the water after 30 minutes. Rinse the inside by running water through one end. Find the end, tie a knot or stick a toothpick through it sideways so you can find it easily. Set it aside.

Toss all of the ingredients together in a mixing bowl and store in the freezer for an hour. Grind with a mixer attachment or pulse quickly with a food processor in small cup-size batches. If you're going wild without any equipment, just remember to chop finely and keep everything cold. The mix should be cohesive and should not fall apart in your hand. Fry a small patty to taste it. Adjust the seasoning, if necessary.

Thread the casing onto a sausage stuffer and slowly fill it with the meat mix. When you've run out of meat, tie off the end with twine. Twist every 6 inches (15 cm) to form the individual sausages. Poke holes with a sewing needle every inch (25 mm) along the whole sausage so it doesn't burst while cooking. If they don't keep their shape, use twine between each sausage to keep them sealed. Hang the sausage rope to dry for 2 hours in a cool place, out of the sun.

Grill on high heat for 2 minutes on each side and finish cooking for 10 minutes on indirect heat until they reach an internal temperature of 150°F (65°C).

Alternatively, poach the sausages in light beer for 7 to 10 minutes until they reach temperature. You can also bake them at 350°F (°C) for 10 minutes.

Let the sausages rest for 5 minutes to solidify and slice on a diagonal.

CHORIZO

MAKES: 1 badass
sausage coil
TOTAL TIME:
4 hours, 15 minutes

Chorizo follows the same method of preparation as the Chinese Sausage (page 55) except that I like to keep this as a single, large coil. It's an impressive sight to behold when you pull this off the grill and present it to your friends on a cutting board with a large knife.

Constituted with crisp Vinho Verde and paprika, this chorizo mix is a little spicy.

---

5 ft (152 cm) sausage casing

2 lb (0.9 kg) pork shoulder, cubed

⅔ lb (300 g) fatback, skin removed and cubed

½ cup (120 ml) cold Vinho Verde or a crisp white wine

4 tsp (22 g) paprika

2 tsp (11 g) salt

3 cloves garlic, minced

2 tsp (11 g) cayenne

1 tsp (6 g) ground cumin

1 tsp (6 g) fresh oregano, chopped

½ tsp freshly ground black pepper

Soak the sausage casing in water. Change the water after 30 minutes. Rinse the inside by running water through one end. Find the end, tie a knot or stick a toothpick through it sideways so you can find it easily. Set it aside.

Toss all of the ingredients together in a mixing bowl and store in the freezer for an hour. Grind with a mixer attachment or pulse quickly with a food processor in small cup-size batches. If you're going wild without any equipment, just remember to chop finely and keep everything cold. The mix should be cohesive and should not fall apart in your hand. Fry a small patty to taste it. Adjust the seasoning, if necessary.

Thread the casing onto a sausage stuffer and slowly fill it with the meat mix. When you've run out of meat, tie off the ends with twine. Poke holes with a sewing needle every inch (25 mm) along the whole sausage so it doesn't burst while cooking. Hang the sausage rope to dry for 2 hours in a cool place, out of the sun.

Grill on high heat for 2 minutes on each side and finish cooking for 10 minutes on indirect heat until it reaches an internal temperature of 150°F (65°C).

Alternatively, poach the sausage in light beer for 7 to 10 minutes until it reaches temperature. You can also bake them at 350°F (177°C) for 10 minutes.

Let the sausage rest for 5 minutes to solidify.

LONGANIZA

MAKES: 20 (3-inch [7-cm]) sausage links
TOTAL TIME:
4 hours, 15 minutes

Longaniza is a Filipino breakfast sausage, twisted into squat, 3-inch (7-cm) pieces. Traditionally it is served *silog* style with a fried egg and a cup of steamed white rice. Again, follow the method of the Chinese Sausage (page 55).

Much mellower then chorizo, longaniza is zestier with lime, tequila and rice vinegar.

5 ft (152 cm) sausage casing

1 guajillo pepper

2 lb (0.9 kg) pork shoulder, cubed

⅔ lb (300 g) fat back, skin removed and cubed

2 tbsp (30 ml) tequila

4 tbsp (20 ml) rice vinegar

1 lime, zested and juiced

2 cloves garlic, minced

1 tsp (6 g) cocoa powder

½ tsp cayenne pepper

2 tsp (11 g) salt

1 tsp (6 g) pepper

Soak the sausage casing in water. Change the water after 30 minutes. Rinse the inside by running water through one end. Find the end, tie a knot or stick a toothpick through it sideways so you can find it easily. Set it aside.

Remove the stem from the guajillo pepper and soak it in warm water for 15 minutes, until it is soft and pliable. Drain the liquid (or use it for another project). Dice the pepper and add it to your mix to grind.

Toss all of the ingredients together in a mixing bowl and store in the freezer for an hour. Grind with a mixer attachment or pulse quickly with a food processor in small cup-size batches. If you're going wild without any equipment, just remember to chop finely and keep everything cold. The mix should be cohesive and should not fall apart in your hand. Fry a small patty to taste it. Adjust the seasoning, if necessary.

Thread the casing onto a sausage stuffer and slowly fill it with the meat mix. When you've run out of meat, tie off the end with twine. Tie off the ends with twine and twist every 3 inches (7 cm) to form the individual sausages. Poke holes with a sewing needle every inch (25 mm) along the whole sausage so it doesn't burst while cooking. If they don't keep their shape, use twine between each sausage to keep them sealed. Hang the sausage rope to dry for 2 hours in a cool place, out of the sun.

Grill on high heat for 2 minutes on each side and finish cooking for 10 minutes on indirect heat until they reach an internal temperature of 150°F (65°C).

Alternatively, poach the sausages in light beer for 7 to 10 minutes until they reach temperature. You can also bake them at 350°F (°C) for 10 minutes.

Let the sausages rest for 5 minutes to solidify.

SPICY LONGANIZA CHAMPORADO

MAKES: **4 to 6 bowls champorado**

TOTAL TIME: **30 minutes**

Up until this point, the competitions had been about featuring one ingredient or one style of food. The Chili-Chocolate Takedown at the Brooklyn Botanic Garden was my first invitational and first challenge using two required ingredients together. I wanted to teach the audience about Filipino food, but I couldn't think of any existing recipe that incorporated both spicy and chocolate elements. I remembered two separate dishes: longaniza and *champorado*.

Longaniza, short pork sausages, are normally eaten *silog* style, with rice. So it's not a far leap to champorado, which is a chocolate rice pudding.

What brings this dish together is the Mexican herb *hoja santa*, a cross between sassafrass and mint. It is available dried in Mexican food aisles and specialty stores.

Olive oil

2 Jamaica or Scotch Bonnet peppers, chopped

1 tsp (6 g) ancho pepper powder

1 clove garlic, grated

2 leaves hoja santa

2 cups (475 ml) chicken broth

1 cup (150 g) sticky rice, uncooked

½ cup + 1 tbsp (45 g + 5 g) dark chocolate, grated

4 links Longaniza (page 58)

Zest 1 lime

In a Dutch oven, sauté the Jamaica peppers, ancho powder, garlic and hoja santa until the garlic is fragrant. Add the chicken broth and bring to a boil. Stir in the rice, cover and cook on medium heat for 15 minutes. Once the rice is tender, turn off the heat and fold in the chocolate.

Pan fry or grill the longaniza for 2 minutes on each side on high heat. Reduce the heat to low and continue to cook for 10 minutes. Turn off the heat and rest for 5 minutes before slicing.

To serve, scoop ¼ cup (53 g) of champorado into a bowl and place a sliced longaniza sausage on top. Finish with a little grated dark chocolate and lime zest.

Winner, Winner Bacon Dinner

After five years of competing in the Takedowns, all of that practice paid off. I came up with a recipe, had time to test it and was strangely serene on the day of the Bacon Takedown (compared to my usual brand of "OMG did I forget tongs?" panic). Hormel gave each entrant coupons equivalent to 15 pounds (6.8 kg) of bacon to use.

When they announced my name as the first place, people's choice winner, I couldn't speak. My voice was hoarse from repeatedly telling people the ingredients during service; I hadn't slept in three days because I was so excited and tending broth.

A new challenge emerged. In addition to prizes like a slate-blue Le Creuset Dutch oven and a spatula trophy, I received "a year's supply of bacon." I imagined Hormel ringing my apartment and plopping a pallet of bacon on my doorstep. Alas, it was less glamorous, with more coupons, but what was I going to do with all of this bacon?

I refer to this time my life as "my year with the pig." In truth, it took me nine months to use it up, but it pushed me to create, create, create.

LESSONS LEARNED

- Save the fat. This was key to my winning dish: by cooking several components of my winning dish in bacon fat, we added a familiar flavor without being wasteful.

- Think outside of the image of breakfast bacon strips. Pick a random dish from a cookbook and imagine how you could incorporate bacon. You might think of surprising combinations!

HOW TO COOK BACON

My year with the pig didn't immediately begin with a year's supply of bacon from the Bacon Takedown. I date it back to a commitment I made during the summer of 2011 to learn how to make charcuterie. You can read recipes from books or from Google search binges, but there is nothing like trying things for yourself, failing, trying them again and succeeding. I cured pancetta in my closet, stuffed my own sausages and ripped apart a whole porcine carcass with my hands. I tried to think back on where my love of pork came from; it must have been the family parties with the intimidating *lechon*, a whole roast pig. Even as picky eater, I'd sneak pieces of the crispy rind, soused with *mang tomas* (Wham Bam Thank You Lamb! [page 140]).

To understand bacon, we must know where it is located on a pig. Bacon comes from the back and sides of our pink-skinned friends, where this is a distinct strip of fat below the skin. Most bacon in stores is cured in salt and smoked, but it is also available uncured. Fat cooks at a different rate than the pink meat itself. Slicing it thinly allows the fat to cook at a similar pace. Thick cuts of bacon need to be cooked at a lower heat and for longer to render the fat from the thicker serving of meat. If you were to fry it on high heat, the fat would be chewy. The pink part of the bacon is a back muscle. When it cooks, it contracts—creating the familiar crinkly constitution.

Stovetop is probably the most common way you will cook bacon. I like to start with a cold cast-iron pan. Place the bacon in a single layer and turn the heat up to medium. If you have room, I actually like to arrange the bacon like a picture frame around where the main flame will be. This way, the bacon cooks evenly. If not, make sure to rotate which pieces get the center flame throughout the cooking process. If you want really crispy bacon, invest in a cast-iron press. It's how diner cooks squish out all that fat. It should only take three to five minutes on each side. If you are cooking multiple batches, make sure to pour off the fat into a jar before you add more bacon to the pan. When you don't, it locks in pockets of fat.

The secret to **baking** whole packs of bacon is to nest a cooling rack inside a lipped baking sheet. This way, the fat drops off the bacon and gathers in the pan below. Half of a pound (227 g) of thick-cut bacon will take about twenty minutes at 350°F (177°C), turning the pan once halfway through. Thinly sliced bacon will take fifteen minutes, depending on how crispy you want it.

On the **grill**, however, the game changes. I prefer to grill whole, uncut slabs of bacon for color and until some of the fat runs off. Then I slice it and finish it again on indirect heat. You will get flare ups as the fat drips down onto the heat source. Make sure you have long enough tongs or say goodbye to your arm hair.

Camping is a little more difficult, too. But it is not impossible! I bring a long cast-iron grill pan and lean it at an angle over a fire with half of it over direct heat and the other half hanging off. That way, the fat drips toward the fire and you can move the bacon off quickly when it flares up. Long tongs, again.

When working with thicker cuts of bacon or slabs, please make sure to cook them until they reach an internal temperature of 160°F (71°C).

WHAT CAN I DO WITH BACON FAT?

When you're cooking a lot of bacon, you're left with a lot of rendered fat. Strain it and keep it in a jar in the fridge for up to two weeks. You can use it to fry eggs, toss with vegetables or brush onto hot rolls and steaks.

It does not do well as a deep frying oil. It has too many solids and will smoke.

BACON VINAIGRETTE

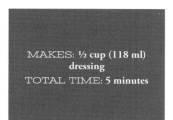

MAKES: ½ cup (118 ml)
dressing
TOTAL TIME: 5 minutes

Bacon fat solidifies in the fridge, so either make this dressing immediately after cooking off bacon or reheat the fat before you begin. Try it with tougher greens like kale, arugula, watercress and frisee. Mesclun greens and lighter leaves will wilt under its weight. Finish a simple salad with a shaving of Parmesan cheese and toasted walnuts. Home fries, potato salad and hearty roasted vegetables can benefit from a lick of fat as well.

Working with fat is a balancing act—you need enough acid, or in this case, lemon to bring it together.

---

4 tbsp (60 ml) strained bacon fat

1 lemon, juiced and zested

½ tsp rice vinegar

2 tsp (11 g) Whole Grain Mustard (page 146)

1 clove garlic, microplaned

¼ tsp salt

½ tsp fresh pepper

Olive oil, optional

Whisk all of the ingredients in a small bowl. Store in a container with a lid in the fridge for up to a week. To use, warm the dressing up in the microwave for 15 to 20 seconds or on the side of the stove while cooking to melt it down.

If you want to tone down the saltiness, add olive oil to your liking.

FATTY FAT TORTILLAS

MAKES: 12 small tortillas
TOTAL TIME: 50 minutes

Flour tortillas are made with lard, and if you're making a lot of bacon, consider a batch of tortillas. I go through them a lot to make brekkie tacos or simply enjoyed as a snack with melted butter and a sprinkle of salt. You can make a lot of these at once and freeze them for later. Also, "Fatty Fat" is one of my nicknames for my brother (who is not fat).

2 cups (250 g) all-purpose flour, plus more for dusting

1 tsp (6 g) baking powder

1 tsp (6 g) kosher salt

¼ cup (60 ml) bacon fat, chilled and solidified

¾ cups (177 ml) cold water

Mix the dry ingredients in a medium bowl. Add the bacon fat and use a whisk to break it up into the flour. Add the water a little bit at a time and stir until the dough sticks itself in one ball. Divide it into twelve small balls. Cover them with plastic wrap or wax paper and let them stand at room temperature for 30 minutes.

Prepare a dry cast iron griddle or pan on high heat.

Dust a cutting board with flour and roll out the balls as thin as you can without breaking them. Cook them in the pan for 20 seconds on each side, they will puff up and brown in some spots. Remove to a plate and insulate with a tea towel. Continue with the rest of the batch.

You can make the balls bigger if you want to make burritos, too.

BACON CHILI OIL

MAKES: **1 pint (473 ml) glorious pork condiment** TOTAL TIME: **15 minutes**

I've tried to figure out the recipe for the Xi'an Famous Foods chili oil by taste. It was legend that only the owner's father knew the recipe, and he was locked in the kitchen while he made it. After trying different combinations and slathering the results all over everything, I knew there was one thing missing—just guess! At that point it didn't really matter if I nailed the original recipe, I much prefer how the salinity marries naturally with the fat toasty sesame taste of tahini and spice.

Blaspheme any grilled vegetables with a spoonful of bacon chili oil, it is especially wonderful between the leaves of a grilled cabbage wedge.

---

1 tsp (6 g) peppercorns

1 tsp (6 g) coriander seeds

1 tbsp (10 g) cumin seeds

2 pieces star anise

2 bay leaves

¼ cup (15 g) chili pepper flakes

4 slices cooked bacon, finely chopped

1 tsp (6 g) curry powder

4 cloves garlic, grated

1 cup (240 ml) vegetable oil

2 tsp (10 ml) soy sauce

1 tbsp (15 ml) tahini

Salt to taste

Combine the peppercorns, coriander seeds, cumin, star anise and bay leaves in a spice grinder. Pulse in short bursts until you make a fine powder. Combine all the ingredients, stirring to incorporate. Taste for desired spiciness and salt. The bacon should be enough salt, but I don't know how much salt you like. If it is too spicy, add more oil. Keep refrigerated and stir before using. The longer the oil sits, the better it will taste. I usually wait a week.

Note: If you prefer to grind your own dried chili peppers, reduce the volume of ¼ cup (60 ml) to a few less peppers. Powdered chili is quite strong. Be careful not to inhale as you open the spice grinder. It will burn your eyes and nose. Trust me, I know.

Don't have a spice grinder? Crush your spices them with a pestle or the blunt handle end of a wooden spoon in a heavy bowl. It's okay, get that aggression out.

WHOSE BACON? NACHO BACON!

MAKES: 4 to 6 servings
TOTAL TIME:
45 minutes active

My winning recipe for the Bacon Takedown is based on a traditionally stewy Filipino dish called *kare-kare*. I managed to transform it into a bite-size bacon peanut curry nacho snack. Gasp—there is no cheese! But don't worry; what we lack in dairy we fully compensate for with pork.

The original kare-kare recipe (adapted from *Memories of Philippine Kitchens* [Besa and Dorotan, 2012]) calls for water. In my test, I noticed that a significant base flavor was missing from the equation. So instead of water, I set out to make my own smoky Tonkotsu Broth (page 37).

½ lb (250 g) thick cut bacon, cooked

1 medium yellow onion

4 cloves garlic

3 plum tomatoes

2 tbsp (30 ml) bacon fat

2 tbsp (30 ml) Ancho Achuete Oil (page 145)

1 quart (950 ml) Tonkotsu Broth (page 37)

8 oz (230 g) chunky peanut butter

3 anchovy fillets

3 bird's eye chilis

½ cup (40 g) green beans, chopped into ¼-inch (6-mm) pieces

1 tbsp (15 ml) sambal

¼ cup (40 g) freeze-dried bananas

⅛ cup (20 g) roasted peanuts, shelled

1 batch Lumpia Chips (page 134)

¼ cup (20 g) fresh cilantro

Chop the bacon into ½-inch (12-mm) pieces.

Make a sofrito by pulsing the onion, garlic and plum tomatoes in a food processor. Add the bacon fat with the ancho oil to a Dutch oven. Cook the sofrito on low heat for 20 minutes, scraping the bottom to avoid burning. Whisk in the tonkotsu broth, peanut butter, anchovy, half of the bacon, chili peppers, green beans and sambal. Cook for 30 minutes.

The slow simmering kare-kare, once cooked, should look like a burnt-sienna crayon with red oily splotches and be thick enough to coat a spoon. You actually want to cool the whole batch down for 20 minutes before you assemble the nachos because they will wilt, and you will be a sad panda without the crispy goodness of the chips. Usually I'd be salting at every step of this journey, but since we're working with bacon, you have to hold back!

Pulverize the bananas with the roasted peanuts in the food processor or with a mortar and pestle. Make sure to use freeze-dried bananas; banana chips will be too sugary, chunky and hard.

To enjoy, take a chip, spoon a tiny bit of kare-kare onto it, throw on a piece of crisp bacon, dust it with a banana peanut powder and top it with a fresh cilantro leaf for brightness. Or if you know you'll be eating it right quick, pile your chips together, spoon peanut curry on and nom it as you please. I can imagine eating this as a dip, too. When you run out of chips (like I did at the Takedown), kare-kare is great over rice, as I originally encountered it growing up.

1ST PLACE, PEOPLE'S CHOICE 2011 BACON TAKEDOWN

SHUMAI, OH MY

MAKES: 20 shumai
TOTAL TIME:
1 hour

Coming off a win from the Bacon Takedown made it difficult to repeat the next year. I wanted to bring something bite-size that I could prepare well ahead of the event. Dim sum proved to be more difficult than I had realized. Any steamed wonton or dumpling material dries as soon as it is exposed to air, which results in a chewy edge. To solve this problem on site, we brought a spritzer bottle to mist the shumai.

To balance out the salty bacon, sake and heavy cream come to the rescue.

¼ lb (115 g) bacon, cooked

¼ cup (40 g) chives, chopped, divided

Sesame seeds

½ lb (250 g) ground pork

½ tbsp (7 ml) sake

½ tbsp (7 ml) heavy cream

1 tbsp (15 ml) soy sauce, plus more for serving

1 tsp (5 ml) bacon fat

1 tbsp (10 g) cornstarch

½ tsp salt

½ tsp white pepper

20 circular wonton wrappers

1 egg

4 large leaves cabbage

Vegetable oil

Chop the bacon finely and divide it into two piles. Mix one with half of the chives and sesame seeds; set aside. Place the rest of the bacon in a mixing bowl with the pork, sake, cream, soy sauce, fat, cornstarch, salt, pepper and remaining chives.

Cover the bowl and place in the fridge for 30 minutes.

Meanwhile, prepare your shumai-making station. Never leave the wonton wrappers exposed to the air, cover them with a damp paper towel to prevent them from drying out. They will crack if you don't keep them pliable.

Lightly beat the egg in a bowl with a splash of water.

Divide the meat mix into 20 balls. To make a shumai, brush a wonton with egg. Place a ball of meat in the center of the wonton. Bring the corners up and start pressing down the folded sides to form a cylinder, as if you had stuffed it into a shot glass. Pat the top of the meat down lightly to fatten it. Continue for the remaining shumai. Top each piece with a generous pinch of the bacon, chive and sesame mix.

Prepare a steamer basket with the leaves of cabbage as your "parchment." Brush the leaves lightly with vegetable oil to prevent the shumai from sticking to the steamer.

Steam for 5 to 8 minutes over 2 inches (5 cm) of boiling water, until the pork reaches an internal temperature of 160°F (71°C).

Enjoy with a side of soy sauce.

CRISPY BACON JIANBING

MAKES: 4 breakfast
jianbing
TOTAL TIME: 25 minutes

I fell in love with a Chinese savory crêpe called *jianbing*. It is an envelope full of egg, crispy wonton and scallion. Because the traditional method is done on large crêpe pans, I opt to fold them in half like a quesadilla. They are an amazing alternative to breakfast burritos or omelets.

If you can find millet flour, replace the all-purpose flour with it. It can be difficult to locate, but it yields a crispier texture!

1 cup (150 g) all-purpose flour

¼ cup (40 g) semolina flour

1 tbsp (15 ml) bacon fat

½ cup (120 ml) soy milk

½ cup (120 ml) soda water

2 tbsp (30 ml) butter, melted

4 eggs

⅛ cup (30 ml) Bacon Chili Oil (page 67)

8 Pickled Chive Buds (page 147), chopped

1 batch Lumpia Chips (page 134)

¼ cup (60 ml) hoisin sauce

⅛ cup (8 g) fried shallots

2 tbsp (5 g) cilantro, chopped

Make the crêpe batter by whisking the flours with the bacon fat, soy milk and water.

Heat a frying pan to medium and brush lightly with butter. Pour in a ½ cup (118 ml) of batter and swirl to cover the pan. Cook the crêpe for 4 minutes until the surface is no longer wet. Lower the heat and crack an egg directly onto the crêpe. Swirl it around with a fork and turn the heat back up. Continue to cook for 2 minutes until the egg is set. Add a spoonful of bacon chili oil, a bit of chive flower and a few lumpia chips. Fold the crêpe in half, remove to a plate and then garnish with hoisin sauce, shallot and cilantro.

Repeat for the remaining 4 crêpes.

MAKE YOUR OWN DAMN BACON

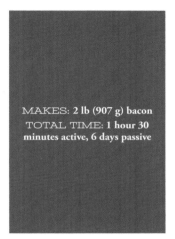

MAKES: **2 lb (907 g) bacon**
TOTAL TIME: **1 hour 30 minutes active, 6 days passive**

The first bacon I made with my own hands was with heritage pork sourced through the Greene Grape. My friend Jake Elmets (now at Ipswich Custom) was the head butcher at the time and helped me get my hands on some pork belly. I largely learned the technique from Michael Ruhlman's *Charcuterie*.

First, we have to make a dry cure. The scary thing about preserving any food is botulism. It's the thing that happens to canned food. Explosions. In the can, in your tummy. Bad bacterial growth. We don't want that! How will this work? The salt crust is going to draw water out of the muscle cells through their semipermeable membranes—meaning some things are allowed in and out of the cell, like a colander but on a molecular scale. Water is allowed, proteins are not. The cell membranes always want to be level. As water comes out of the meat, the flavors of the other things in the bag will go in to balance everything out. Science!

The coolest part of making your own damn bacon is deciding how thick, sweet or salty you want it to be.

---

1 tsp (6 g) black peppercorns

1 tsp (6 g) coriander seeds

4 tbsp (80 g) kosher salt

2 tbsp (23 g) brown sugar

½ tbsp (3 g) pink curing salt

3 cloves garlic, grated

2 bay leaves

3 lb (1.2 kg) slab fresh pork belly

¼ cup (60 ml) maple sugar or syrup

Place all the dry ingredients in a large zip top bag, hold it closed and shake it to mix everything together. If you don't have a bag, any shallow-lipped nonreactive container will do, as long as the pork can soak in it.

Add the pork and maple syrup (if you're using) to the bag. Seal the bag and spread the mix around. Nest the bag on a baking sheet before you put it in the fridge, just in case it leaks.

After two days, flip the belly and move the cure around, making sure it is covered. Wait two more days and flip again. Repeat for another round, making it a total of 6 days to cure. Feel the thickest part of the belly for squishiness. If it is squishy, continue to cure. Otherwise, if it feels dense, it is done.

Rinse off the brine and pat the belly dry with paper towels.

Smoke the belly on indirect heat for 2 to 3 hours, until the internal temperature reaches 150°F (65°C). If you want to dry the bacon in the oven, simply roast it on a rack at 250°F (121°C) until it reaches the desired temperature.

While it is still hot, you can remove the skin if you don't prefer to have the rind on. Some folks don't like chewing on it. Use the rind for Hot Ham Water Dashi (page 35) or Tonkotsu Broth (page 37).

Slice off a piece and fry it to test. If it is too salty, you can blanch and dry it before frying. If it is not salty enough, by all means, add more salt!

You can precut your bacon and store it in the fridge for up to a week or freeze it up to three months.

BACON TARTINE

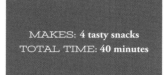

MAKES: 4 tasty snacks
TOTAL TIME: 40 minutes

After I had made my own bacon, this was a hidden item on a Project Parlor menu. I only told two people and word got around throughout the day. The arugula salad cuts through the bacon fat and the beer cheese just melts when it hits the grilled bread. Fried garlic is available in big buckets at Asian specialty markets, but here, we'll make it at home.

If you can't fine filone, any grillable French style bread will work. Don't forget the fried garlic chips!

---

8 slices thick-cut bacon

½ lb (250 g) arugula

1 lemon, juiced and tested

1 tsp (6 g) salt

Pepper

4 (1½-inch [38-mm]) slices crusty filone bread

½ cup (120 ml) Grown-Up Handi-Snacks (page 173)

1 tsp (5 ml) olive oil

1 cup (240 ml) vegetable oil

1 head of garlic, peeled

Grill the bacon on high for 2 minutes and then move to indirect heat for 5 to 7 minutes.

Toss the arugula with the lemon juice, salt and pepper. Quickly grill the bread for 30 seconds each side, enough to get the grill marks. Spread the beer cheese on each slice of bread, top with two slices of finished bacon and a few strands of lemon zest.

In a small saucepan, heat the vegetable oil on medium heat for 3 minutes. Meanwhile, slice the garlic as thinly as possible. Submerge the garlic in the oil and fry it so the edges of the garlic are bubbling. Cook for 1 minute and shut off the heat. Let the garlic bubble from the residual heat for 20 minutes. Strain the garlic out and dry it on paper towels. Reserve the garlic oil for another project.

Sprinkle 1 tablespoon (10 g) of the fried garlic over both the tartine and salad.

PEANUT CURRY MAZEMEN

MAKES: **2 hearty noodle bowls**

TOTAL TIME: **15 minutes**

Mazemen is a type of Japanese ramen with a reduced sauce. Use leftover Whose Bacon? Nacho Bacon! (page 68) here.

The clean flavor of cilantro will cut through the thick, fatty curry.

1 pack cheap ramen noodles

2 cups (475 ml) Whose Bacon? Nacho Bacon! (page 68)

2 eggs, soft boiled

½ tsp sesame seeds

2 or 3 stems cilantro leaves

Boil the ramen noodles for 2 minutes in water, drain.

Prepare two soup bowls with a cup (240 ml) of hot curry each. Divide the noodles between them and top with an egg. Garnish with a smattering of sesame seeds and a tuft of cilantro leaves.

HOMEMADE TASSO

MAKES: **2 lb (0.9 kg) tasso**
TOTAL TIME: **10 minutes active, 8 hours passive**

Tasso is routinely found in southern food like jambalaya or as a base for stewed vegetables. It is fatty pork shoulder that is cured, then crusted in a warm spice mix of allspice and marjoram.

7 tbsp (140 g) salt

1 tsp (6 g) pink curing salt

3½ tbsp (40 g) brown sugar

2 lb (0.9 kg) boneless pork shoulder

¼ cup (40 g) fine bread crumbs

1 tbsp (5 g) white pepper

1 tbsp (5 g) marjoram

1 tbsp (5 g) allspice

¼ tsp ghost pepper powder or ½ tsp chili powder of your choice

Liquid smoke, optional

Combine the salts and sugar in a shallow pan, mix it together lightly.

Slice the pork into 1-inch (25-mm) thick steaks and pat them dry with a paper towel.

Press the pork in the curing salt mixture, making sure to coat all sides thickly. Lift the meat out carefully and place in another pan; discard the unused salt cure. Cover the pan with plastic wrap and cure overnight in the refrigerator.

Meanwhile, combine the bread crumbs with the remaining spices to make a dry rub.

Remove the pork from the fridge, wash each piece and pat dry with a paper towel. Coat each piece with a generous amount of the dry rub.

If you have a smoker, hot smoke with applewood chips to an internal temperature of 160°F (71°C).

If not, preheat the oven to 135°F (57°C). Place the pork on a rack nested in a sheet pan. Dry the pork for an hour with the oven door cracked open with a wooden spoon. Fill a food-safe spray bottle with 1 part liquid smoke to 4 parts water.

Remove the wooden spoon and raise the temperature to 175°F (80°C). Cook to an internal temperature of 160°F (71°C), approximately 3 or 4 hours. Spray the pork with the liquid smoke mixture 3 or 4 times. Let the surface dry each time, so you don't wash the spices off the meat.

If you don't have a spray bottle, fill a small ramekin with the smoke liquid and place it on the lowest rack of the oven.

The tasso should be dense, but not dry and brittle like jerky. Let it cool completely before storing.

Light It Up

I'll say it now. I'm no pitmaster. I was having a drink in 2010 at a newly opened bar called Project Parlor in Brooklyn. At the time, owner Megyn Florence was tending the bar and telling someone else about a BBQ competition she wanted to start in the backyard that summer. I gave away my eavesdropping and asked if she could include me. I thought it would be fun to meet the neighbors. How hard could this be?

Oh, wow, I was wrong. The Project Parlor BBQ championship was a commitment. Sixteen teams went head-to-head in a bracket-style tournament every Sunday for the whole summer. Each team had to come up with a full menu, and whoever made the most money between 2 p.m. and 9 p.m. went to the next round. This was nothing like the Takedowns.

It was 90°F (32°C) outside, and I was standing over the blazing fire, holding a "Man-mosa" (Project Parlor staple, a pint mimosa). Jeff grunted as he hauled a second bag of charcoal from our grocery cart onto the ground. We didn't realize we had to manage orders and money on top of cooking it all. It was a tough summer.

We nervously counted our money for three rounds and made it to the finals. We crushingly lost to Theo and Deb of Pearl Lee Q's catering. The next year, we were knocked out in the second round and got sixth place. Megyn had faith that our day would come, and it happened. Jeff and I were crowned the 2012 BBQ champions. Not only did we get a 7-foot (2-m)-tall trophy, we generated three years of completely thought-out catering menus.

LESSONS LEARNED

- Practice starting a fire and lighting coals with and without a chimney. You lose grilling time if you can't get it correct right away.

- It's tempting to be "meat-minded" when you think of grilling and barbecue. An accommodating menu considers price point affordability, complimentary flavors, portion size and specialty diet options like vegetarian, vegan and gluten-free. Knowing every single ingredient in your dishes can also inform allergy warnings.

- It's hard to prep for an event when you don't know how many people will show up. Project as best you can and think of how many total orders you can confidently sell, and work backwards from there. Observe attendance for next time if it's a repeat event.

- We noticed recurring items that we needed for every round of the championship, so we started a kit (see Tools and Travel Kit, page 180).

SMOKING VEGETABLES AND FRUITS

Living in Brooklyn has its perks with regard to food waste. At every farmers market and some community gardens, you can bring your vegetable scraps to be composted. I don't have the space to have my own compost bin or the land to use it on when it is finished. For bits and bobs that cannot be used for broth, I air-dry and use them for new flavors in my smoker.

In a sunny window sill, I age mushroom stems or twiggy herb stems in a single layer on a small sheet pan. Do not pile them or you can trap moisture that can promote mold.

Tie leftover herbs or vegetable tops (like dill, radish greens and fennel fronds) into bunches with twine and hang them to dry for a day or two.

CARNE ASADA

MAKES: 2 lb (907 g) steak
TOTAL TIME: 20 minutes
active, up to 8 hours passive

Many California transplants like myself complain that there is no good Mexican food in New York City. The hard concept to swallow is that it is merely different and hidden in faraway food trucks, or the back of bodegas where the carne asada is grilled fresh for waiting tortillas. This is my homesick way to bring back that feeling like I'm back home in California, eating a delicious street taco after a night out at a bar with friends.

Carne asada gets its signature punchy flavor from a mix of lime, honey and smoky ancho pepper.

¼ cup (60 ml) olive oil

¼ cup (60 ml) soy sauce

2 tbsp (30 ml) white vinegar

1 tsp (5 ml) honey

2 limes juiced and zested

1 orange, juiced and zested

4 garlic cloves, grated

1 tbsp (10 g) ancho chili powder

1 tbsp (10 g) ground cumin

1 jalapeño, seeded and minced

Salt and pepper to taste

2 lb (900 g) flank steak

2 tbsp (20 g) fresh oregano

2 tbsp (20 g) fresh cilantro

Whisk all of the wet ingredients in a mixing bowl. Stir in the citrus zests, garlic, ancho, cumin and jalapeño.

Lightly salt and pepper the steak on both sides in a lipped sheet pan. Pour the marinade over the steak and cover with plastic for 2 hours. Flip the steaks and cover with a fresh sheet of plastic wrap. Marinate for 2 more hours or up to 8 total.

Grill on high heat, 4 minutes on each side, until a thermometer reads 155°F (68°C). Let the steak rest for 3 minutes in a new lipped sheet pan to collect the juices. Slice the steak into thirds with the grain and then rotate each piece to cut against the grain. Garnish the slices with the meat juices, oregano and cilantro.

Alternatively, heat a grill pan on high on the stove. Open a window or turn on yout microwave vent to suck up the smoke. Proceed to cook as directed.

PROJECT PARLOR
2012 SUMMER BBQ
COMPETITION
WINNER

PULLED CHICKEN MOLE

MAKES: 4 large servings or
8 sandwich servings

TIME: 1 hour

We wanted to run with the idea of grilled sandwiches during the Project Parlor competition, and Jeff really loved tortas. Making them on the grill instead of in the kitchen seemed especially challenging. I'll never forget Jeff's broken Spanish as we ordered *auténtico* torta rolls from a bodega on Myrtle Avenue in Brooklyn, *"¡Cuarenta, si! Cuarenta."* They wouldn't believe that we wanted forty pieces of bread. When we went to pick it up, they were in a giant trash bag.

Soft, juicy chicken awaits you in a spicy, nutty sauce.

---

4 bone-in skin-on chicken breasts

3 cups (700 ml) chicken stock

2 dried ancho chiles

1 chipotle pepper in adobo sauce, minced

¼ tsp ground cinnamon

⅛ tsp ground cloves

¼ cup (60 ml) chunky nut butter

¼ cup (40 g) dates

2 tbsp (30 ml) tahini

3 medium shallots, minced

3 tbsp (45 ml) vegetable oil

2 cloves garlic, smashed

1 (14½-oz [440-ml]) can diced tomatoes, drained

2½ tbsp (30 g) dark chocolate, chopped

Salt

Pepper

Place the chicken in a pot and cover with the stock, bring to a boil. Lower to a simmer and cook for 30 to 40 minutes until the meat is tender and has an internal temperature of 165°F (74°C). Drain and save the broth, set the chicken aside.

Using the already-boiling stock, reconstitute the dried chili peppers in the pot. Carefully fish them out with tongs when they are soft. Remove the stems and place in the bowl of a food processor with the chipotle, cinnamon, clove, nut butter, dates and tahini. Pulse until the larger pieces are broken and blend on low until it forms a smooth paste.

In a large pan, sauté the shallots in vegetable oil until they soften for 3 minutes. Add the garlic and cook for a minute more before adding the tomatoes. Break up the tomatoes with a wooden spoon and add the spiced paste from the food processor.

Cook for 15 minutes on medium, until the liquid cooks off. Strain 1 cup (240 ml) of the chicken broth cooking liquid into the sauce and stir. Just like risotto, as the liquid cooks off, add another cup of the chicken broth, until you have one left. At that point, take it off the heat and stir in the chocolate. Season to taste with the salt and pepper.

As the sauce cooks, cool the chicken and debone it. Pull the chicken apart, making sure no pieces are bigger than the width of your thumb.

Fold the meat into the sauce and serve immediately, or if you're not eating just yet, add the last of the broth and cover. Keep warm in the oven at 200°F (93°C) until you're ready to eat.

If you're eating later, cool the mixture down and store in the fridge overnight. An hour before serving, add the remaining chicken broth before heating it back up.

PROJECT PARLOR
2012 SUMMER BBQ
COMPETITION
WINNER

CHICKEN MOLE TORTA

MAKES: 4 tortas
TOTAL TIME: 10 minutes

My tortas are a tribute to the stacked *torta de salchicha* you can find in the back of the Puebla Mini Mart in Sunset Park, Brooklyn. One particularly lonely Valentine's Day, Jeff, Angela and I ventured to eat these sandwiches. With our favorite bottles of grapefruit Jarritos soda, we tackled these beasts. Who needed a Valentine when you could have the biggest sandwich, ever?

Are you ready for a flavor explosion in your face? Nutty, spicy chicken slathered with warm cinnamon bean spread, crunchy lettuce and creamy avocado are what makes this torta legendary.

4 torta rolls

RECOMMENDED
FILLINGS

1 cup (160 g) Pulled Chicken Mole (page 86)

¼ cup (80 g) Black Bean Spread (page 154)

¼ head shredded iceberg lettuce

¼ cup (60 ml) Cher-Meow-La (page 151)

1 sliced avocado

¼ cup (180 g) crumbled queso fresco

2 sliced radishes

IF YOU WANT TO
GO NUTS IN TRUE
DAGWOOD STYLE,
PILE ON THE
FOLLOWING

2 hot dogs, sliced lengthwise and in half

4 slices bacon

4 slices ham

4 fried eggs

First you have to find a bodega that carries this particularly wonderful torta bread referred to as *bolillo*, *telera* or *birote*. It looks like a football, crusty on the outside and fluffy on the inside. It toasts really well, like a cubano.

Slice the torta rolls in half and toast them on a dry pan for 2 minutes, cut side down.

Warm the chicken in a microwave-safe bowl for 2 minutes or bring to a simmer in a saucepan for 5 minutes.

To assemble, spread 1 spoonful of Black Bean Spread onto the bottom of the roll and 1 spoonful of Cher-Meow-La on the top of the roll. Using tongs, place ¼ cup (80 g) of Chicken Mole over the beans, add a small handful of lettuce, then 2 or 3 slices of avocado. Crumble a few pinches of queso before crowning the sandwich with the top bun. Skewer 2 pieces of sliced radish through the whole torta.

PROJECT PARLOR
2012 SUMMER BBQ
COMPETITION
WINNER

GRILLED FLAKEY FLATBREAD

MAKES: 8 flatbreads
TOTAL TIME: 10 minutes active, 5 hours passive

Flatbread is versatile. You can eat it with dips, roll it up with sandwich fillings or even treat it like a thin crust pizza. This recipe is worth the time and effort. You can prepare the dough ahead of time and store it in the freezer for grilling season.

If you can't find crema, replace it with sour cream.

2½ tsp (14 g) active dry yeast

3 cups (709 ml) warm water

6 cups (720 g) all-purpose flour, plus more for dusting

½ cup (120 ml) Mexican crema

1 tsp (5 ml) honey

2 tbsp (20 g) Tomato Salt (page 158)

¼ cup (60 ml) olive oil

¼ cup (60 ml) butter, melted

2 sprigs dill

Stir the yeast with warm water in a large mixing bowl. Add the flour gradually and run it through your fingers until it barely comes together. Cover the bowl with a clean towel at room temperature for 25 minutes.

Add the crema, honey and tomato salt and knead the dough for 4 to 7 minutes, until it is a moist ball that doesn't stick to the bowl. Cover the bowl again and let the dough rise for another 30 minutes.

Punch the dough and fold it in half 3 times. Let the dough rise for up to 4 hours, when it doubles in size. Smack the dough down one more time and chill in the fridge for an hour.

Roll out 8 flatbreads on a floured surface. Make them as flat as you can, then roll them into cigars. Loop the cigar into a cinnamon roll and then flatten that out to ¼ inch (6 mm) thickness. It's okay if they're not perfectly circular; they're charming when they're the shape of unfamiliar countries.

Brush the grill with olive oil and cook the flatbreads for up to 2 to 3 minutes on each side; they will naturally unstick themselves if you cook them long enough. Serve warm with a brush of butter and a sprinkle of dill.

PROJECT PARLOR
2012 SUMMER BBQ
COMPETITION
WINNER

ROASTED STUFFED POBLANO FLATBREAD

MAKES: 8 stuffed peppers
TOTAL TIME: 40 minutes
active, 10 minutes passive

Chile rellenos were a hearty vegetarian option we came up with during the Project Parlor championship. Instead of making a tofu sandwich version of whatever our meat was, we thought this was way more exciting for our friends. The addition of the flatbread wrapped around it cut down on the use of utensils (another cost that racks up pretty quickly if you don't pay attention).

If you are short on time, you can substitute the flatbread with big flour tortillas, simply kissed on the flame of the grill to warm them up.

While poblanos are a mild pepper, the satisfying filling and flatbread are elevated by chermoula—a zinging sauce of mint, cilantro and ginger.

---

1 tsp (6 g) cumin seeds, toasted

2 tbsp (30 ml) butter

1 onion

1 cup (150 g) brown rice, uncooked

1½ cups (360 ml) vegetable broth

8 medium poblano peppers

1 cup (150 g) cooked black beans

¼ cup (40 g) pepitas

2 medium tomatoes, chopped

½ cup (40 g) chopped cilantro

1 cup (150 g) crumbled cotija cheese, divided

3 tsp (16 g) salt

1 jalapeño, chopped

¾ cup (180 ml) Mexican crema

8 Grilled Flakey Flatbreads (page 88)

¼ cup (90 ml) Chermoula (page 150)

Toast the cumin on medium heat in a dry Dutch oven until fragrant for 1 minute. Add the butter and onion, then sauté until they are translucent and softened for 3 minutes. Put in the rice and toast for a minute. Turn the heat up to high flame and pour in the broth. Bring it to a boil and then reduce to low heat and cover with a lid for 20 minutes. Turn off the heat.

While the rice cooks, chop the stems off the poblano peppers and remove the seeds by scraping them out with a spoon. Tap the peppers on a cutting board to get any loose seeds that may be hiding. Set the peppers aside.

Once the rice is cooked, let it cool with the lid off for 10 minutes. In a large bowl, mix the rice with the black beans, pepitas, tomato, cilantro and all but ¼ cup (30 g) of cotija cheese. Taste the mix and season with the salt to your liking.

Quickly grill the empty peppers on high, enough to get a couple grill marks on both sides but not enough that they soften. Prepare 8 pieces of foil that will cover each pepper. Stuff the peppers with the rice mix and wrap in the foil.

Store them on indirect heat while you grill tortillas or flatbreads. Brush each finished flatbread with chermoula. When you're ready to serve, move the foil packs to direct heat and cook in each side for 3 minutes.

Be careful when you open the foil packs; steam will escape. To serve, place a pepper on a flatbread or tortilla, drizzle a little crema and then dust with a generous pinch of cotija cheese.

PROJECT PARLOR 2012 SUMMER BBQ COMPETITION WINNER

POBLANO FRIED RICE

MAKES: A yummy
breakfast for two
TOTAL TIME: 15 minutes

In my household growing up, any leftovers from dinner were chopped and tossed in a fried rice the next morning. If you have a couple stuffed peppers left, this is a quick way to repurpose them.

You can buy fried shallots from Asian specialty stores.

2 leftover stuffed poblanos or 2 cups (322 g), Roasted Stuffed Poblano rice mix (page 91)

1 tbsp (15 ml) butter

1 clove garlic, sliced

1 tbsp (15 ml) salsa or hot sauce

1 handful hearty greens like arugula or kale

⅛ cup (8 g) fried shallot

Chop the poblanos into rings and break the rice up with a spoon.

Melt the butter in a pan on medium heat. Add the garlic and sauce until the edges sizzle. Put in the poblano rice and sauté for a 2 minutes to coat the rice in butter. Add the salsa and stir to coat. The rice is done frying after 8 to 10 minutes when you don't have clumps and the grains have a buttery shine on them. Turn the heat off and fold in the greens. They will steam on their own from the heat.

Top with the fried shallot and enjoy. It's an excellent hangover cure, I know from experience.

BROOKLYN BULGOGI

Korean barbecue was a treat with my family. It was a special time because all 22 of us cousins, aunts and uncles rarely saw each other and would take over the whole wing of a restaurant.

I loved my little pair of tongs and moving all of the spicy *bulgogi* around on the sizzling surface. The most interesting discovery in some Korean marinades is the use of fruit; the acid breaks the meat down and lends an amount of sugar that caramelizes as you grill it. Use an apple pear or Asian pear, but if you can't find one, use your favorite kind of apple or pear!

At some specialty markets you can buy presliced bulgogi meat, but you can also do it yourself.

MAKES: 4 servings
TOTAL TIME: 25 minutes
active, 5 hours passive

1½ lb (675 g) beef sirloin

1 apple pear

1 cup (240 ml) sake

½ cup (120 ml) soy sauce

½ cup (120 ml) ginger beer

¼ cup (45 g) brown sugar

4 cloves garlic, smashed

¼ cup (40 g) shallot, chopped

⅛ cup (30 ml) sesame oil

1 tsp (6 g) salt

1 tbsp (10 g) white pepper

¼ cup (60 ml) bacon fat

2 tbsp (20 g) sesame seeds

4 scallions, chopped into rings

2 cups (322 g) cooked white rice

4 bao buns, for serving

8 butter lettuce leaves, for serving

Freeze the sirloin for an hour to make it easier to slice. Lay the steak horizontally on your cutting board. Cut it vertically into thirds. Rotate a piece 90 degrees and then cut against the muscle grain as thinly as possible. This will make it easier to chew after you cook it. Repeat with the remaining 2 pieces.

Peel, core and grate the apple pear. Combine it with the sake, soy sauce, ginger beer, sugar, garlic, shallot, sesame oil, salt and white pepper. Marinate the steak for at least 2 hours or up to 4.

Prepare a grill with a heat-safe cooling rack on top. Since the meat is sliced so thinly, it could fall between the spaces of a normal gridiron. Brush the grill surfaces with melted bacon fat.

Cook the beef on high heat for 20 seconds on each side. They will cook very quickly.

If you want to try this indoors, make sure you have great ventilation or a window with a fan pointing outward.

Heat a clean cast-iron grill pan in the oven on the highest setting for 30 minutes (a trick I learned from Grant Achatz). If you have anything stuck on the pan or at the bottom of your oven, you will know immediately by the thick cloud of smoke that emerges, hence the ventilation. While you wait, prepare the table with at least three layers of trivets, cutting boards you don't care about or pot holders. The cast iron will be so hot that it will brand your table if you do not provide enough insulation.

Alternatively you can use a panini grill that opens completely flat. It provides constant heat and has gutters to catch any juices that gather on the pan.

Brush the grill surface with bacon fat. Use tongs to place the beef on your heat source and flip once after 30 seconds. Guests can remove cooked beef with chopsticks or forks, but make sure not to cross contaminate the raw beef with the cooked.

Eat the beef with your choice of rice, bao bun or simply wrapped in lettuce leaves.

Reserve the marinade for the Korean Dip (page 98).

PROJECT PARLOR
2012 SUMMER BBQ
COMPETITION
WINNER

KOREAN SUB

**MAKES: 4 full sandwiches
or 8 snacks
TOTAL TIME: 5 minutes**

As part of the Project Parlor championship, we decided to make the Korean BBQ experience available on a sandwich! Omit the Whipped Ssamjang and Kimchi Apples if you are averse to spicy foods.

In one bite you will get tasty caramelized beef, crisp green apple and the rage of spicy ssamjang, calmed by a cooling wave of creamy yogurt.

4 sub rolls

4 leaves romaine lettuce

1 lb (0.5 kg) cooked Brooklyn Bulgogi beef (page 93)

½ cup (75 g) Kimchi Apples (page 157)

4 Pickled Chive Buds (page 147)

¼ cup (60 ml) Whipped Ssamjang (page 152)

¼ cup (60 ml) Savory Yogurt (page 152)

Sesame seeds

Split the sub rolls in half, leaving a hinge. Scoop out the fluffy insides, eat them or save for bread crumbs later. Nest a romaine leaf in the hollow of the bread and place the beef in the curve of the lettuce. On the other side, layer 2 or 3 kimchi apple slices and one chive flower stalk. If you have your sauces in squeeze bottles, make mirrored lines across the top of the sandwich with the ssamjang and the yogurt. If you don't have squeeze bottles, spread the sauces on opposite sides of the bread before filling it.

Sprinkle a bit of sesame seeds on top to finish.

PROJECT PARLOR
2012 SUMMER BBQ
COMPETITION
WINNER

CRUNCHY ELOTE

MAKES: 4 whole ears of
corn or 8 half portions
TOTAL TIME: 20 minutes
active, 2 hours passive

Elote is already a wonderful Mexican street dish consisting of luscious crema slathered on an ear of corn and rolled in a mixture of Parmesan cheese and cayenne pepper. The addition of pork rinds adds a devilish amount of fat and texture to each kernel popping bite. For my vegetarian friends, substitute the rinds for fried crispy shallots and/or garlic.

4 ears corn

1 small (4-oz [112-g]) bag pork rinds

⅓ cup (80 ml) crema

1 lime, juiced and zested

½ tsp cayenne pepper

⅛ cup (11 g) grated Parmesan cheese

Pull off any silk from the end of each ear of corn and cut off the opposite hard, stalky end. Submerge the ears in salted water for at least 2 hours. Use a plate to weigh them down. Grill in the coals or over direct gas grill heat for 8 to 10 minutes. It's okay that the husks burn off a little.

To save time, you can also parboil shucked corn for 10 minutes, until the kernels are bright yellow. Alternatively, you can cook in-husk corn directly on the oven rack at 350°F (177°C) for 30 to 40 minutes, or until the corn is soft to the touch.

While the corn cooks, pulse the pork rinds in a food processor or crush them in a zipped plastic bag. Discard any hard rinds that don't break down. Combine the crema with the lime juice, zest and cayenne pepper. On a baking sheet, toss the pork rinds with the Parmesan cheese.

To finish, remove the corn husks (if you haven't already), use a spatula to spread the crema onto each ear and roll it in the pan of crunchy rinds.

Consume immediately. The pork rinds become soggy if they are left to sit.

KOREAN DIP

MAKES: 4 large sandwiches
or 8 appetizer portions
TOTAL TIME: 15 minutes

I love French dip sandwiches. If you think about it, bulgogi is like a flavor-packed version of chipped beef for cheesesteak!

Enter: a hyped-up beef broth that utilizes the leftover marinade.

1 tbsp (15 ml) leftover marinade from cooking the bulgogi

1 pint (475 ml) beef broth

1 tbsp (15 ml) butter

4 French bread rolls or baguette

8 slices provolone or jack cheese

1 lb (0.5 kg) Brooklyn Bulgogi beef (page 93)

Bring the marinade to a boil in a pot with the beef broth. Boil for 3 minutes and lower to a simmer. Cook for 10 minutes on low. Strain the broth into a heat-safe bowl, add the butter and store in the microwave or warm oven until you are ready to eat.

Split the rolls in half, leaving a hinge. Layer 2 slices of cheese on one side and then pile on the beef. Wrap each sandwich in foil and place in a warm oven or on indirect grill heat until the cheese melts for 5 to 7 minutes.

Divide the broth or "jus" into four ramekins or bowls. Dip your melty sandwich into the broth and take a bite. The bread should soak it up and squish in your mouth (in the most exciting way possible).

MISO CURRY ONIGIRI

One of my favorite textures in this world is the crisped up rice at the bottom of a Korean *bibimbap*. I discovered that in Japanese cuisine, you can order these as snacks! *Onigiri* is traditionally a steamed rice ball wrapped in seaweed or grilled with soy sauce. We came up with this idea for a Project Parlor round to have a side dish that did not require utensils.

Most grilled rice balls are brushed with a diluted solution of miso and water. The curry adds a complex, lemongrassy and hot twist to the Japanese Izakaya favorite.

If you have leftovers, you can break up the balls and make fried rice.

Nori are seaweed sheets, found in Japanese food aisles or specialty stores.

MAKES: 4 rice balls or 8 if you scoop ½-cup (80-g) servings
TOTAL TIME: 1 hour

2 cups (380 g) sushi rice
3 cups (700 ml) water
1 tbsp (15 ml) red curry paste
1 tsp (6 g) white miso
1 tsp (5 ml) soy sauce
Kosher salt
Olive oil
2 sheets of nori, sliced in half for serving, optional

Rinse the sushi rice in cold water. Set it to cook with the 3 cups (700 ml) of water in a rice cooker. If you don't have a rice cooker, bring the rice and 3 cups (700 ml) of water to a boil in a pot. Once it is boiling, cover with a lid and reduce to a simmer for 20 minutes.

While you wait, whisk the curry paste with the miso and soy sauce.

Once the rice is done, remove the lid and use a wooden spoon to chop through the rice 3 or 4 times while fanning it with a magazine or piece of cardboard. Wait until the rice has cooled enough to handle bare-handed.

Rub a little salt on your hands and scoop 1 cup (190 g) of rice. Cup your hands over the rice into 90° angles. Your fingertips from your right hand should be touching your left thumb and your left fingertips should be touching your right pinky knuckle. Pretend you are catching lightning bugs, but instead you are packing rice lightly into a triangle shape. Do not let the rice completely cool or it will not stick together.

Prepare an oiled grill or cast iron pan on medium heat. Baste the onigiri with the curry sauce every 2 minutes and cook on all sides for 15 minutes until browned and crispy.

To save time, you can also brush the rice balls with the curry sauce and simply wrap a half-sheet of nori around it like a sandwich.

"I LIKE IT SHALLOT" BURGER

MAKES: 6 (⅓-lb [150-g]) or 8 (¼-lb [113-g]) burgers
TOTAL TIME: 1 hour active, 30 minutes passive

The idea of this burger mix came from James Beard via another cook named Jeanne Owen. Originally, you grated onion into the meat. I like to use the less intense flavor of shallots with the smoky flavor of paprika. Instead of using burger buns that get soggy halfway through eating them, I took a page from Prune's Gabrielle Hamilton, who uses English muffins for her burgers. They're sturdy and toast up well.

2 lb (900 g) ground round beef

2 tbsp (30 ml) heavy cream

2 small shallots, grated

1 garlic clove, grated

2 tsp (11 g) salt

1 tsp (6 g) paprika

1 tbsp (15 ml) unsalted butter, melted

6 slices white cheddar cheese

⅓ cup (80 ml) Meyer Lemon Mayo (page 153)

⅓ cup (80 ml) Romantic Romesco (page 154)

6 English muffins

6 slices tomato

6 leaves Boston lettuce

Wavy potato chips, optional

Combine the beef, heavy cream, shallot, garlic, salt and paprika. Fold the mixture delicately, careful not to overwork the meat. It is okay if it is studded visibly with shallot. Cover the bowl with plastic wrap and place in the refrigerator for at least an hour.

Using gloved hands, toss the meat one more time and then form 6 evenly-sized patties. Using your thumb, dent each burger with your thumb and then pinch from the center around the edges, as if you're making a really shallow ash tray.

Preheat the oven to 200°F (93°C).

Prepare a grill with a hot side and a cool side for resting burgers. Grill the burgers for 2 minutes and brush with butter. Flip and grill for 4 minutes, brush with more butter.

Rest the burgers on the cool side of the grill and place a slice of cheese on each one or store them on a sheet pan in the oven. Spread Meyer Lemon Mayo on one half of English muffin and toast on the grill. Assemble like so: bread, a spoonful of Romesco, cheese, burger, tomato, lettuce and bread. Enjoy with a bag of wavy chips; those are my favorite to have with burgers.

VARIATION: SMASHED ON THE STOVETOP

I love In-N-Out and smashed burgers. There's something about the increased surface area that yields more crisp potential. Plus it's really fun to smash something on a hot surface. Makes you feel all-powerful.

Place a cast-iron pan on high heat. Instead of forming a meat mix, form 6 large meatballs. Replace the butter with clarified butter or ghee. It cooks better at high heat and doesn't burn as much. Beware of flare-ups near the edge of the pan. Turn on your vent; this dish will smoke!

Before cooking, brush the pan quickly with butter and then put in the meatball. Smash it down on the hot grill as flat as you can with a spatula or iron press. Cook for 2 minutes and then carefully flip it. Finish in the pan for another 2 minutes. Assemble and devour.

BAA-DAASS BURGER

MAKES: 4 burgers
TOTAL TIME: up to
4 hours passive

Cumin and lamb go so well together. I wanted to convert my favorite Sichuan style stir-fry dish into a sandwich. The spices in this burger pack a punch. If you don't like spicy food, omit the ancho powder and slather on a spoonful of yogurt to cool it off. However, I really enjoy this burger with an additional kick of Bacon Chili Oil (page 67).

1 lb (0.5 kg) ground lamb

1 medium shallot, minced

2 cloves garlic, grated

½ tsp coriander seeds, crushed

½ tsp ancho pepper powder

1 tsp (5 ml) heavy cream

1 tsp (5 ml) apple brandy

1 tsp (5 ml) soy sauce

1 tsp (6 g) ground cumin

1 tbsp (10 g) salt

2 tbsp (30 ml) butter, divided into 4 pieces

4 English muffins

¼ cup (40 ml) plain yogurt, for serving, optional

Combine everything but the butter and muffins in a medium mixing bowl. Carefully fold the ingredients together, making sure not to overwork it. Refrigerate for an hour or up to 4. Divide the meat into 4 balls.

Split and toast your English muffins on indirect grill heat. Shape the meatballs into 1-inch (25-mm) thick discs. They will shrink on the grill. As you place the burgers on the grill, make a quick divot in the center with your thumb and place a pat of butter in each one. Make sure it is melted before you flip. Cook for 4 minutes on each side or until their internal temperatures read 160°F (71°C).

Alternatively, split and toast your English muffins in the oven. Then reduce the oven to a holding temperature of 200°F (93°C). Heat a cast-iron pan on high. Just before you put in a meatball, throw in a pat of butter and then smash the burger on top of it with a spatula, to 1-inch (25-mm) thickness. Cook for 3 minutes on each side, or at least up to an internal temperature of 160°F (71°C). Store the burgers in the oven until you are ready to serve with a dollop of yogurt.

"I NEED THAT SLOPPY"

MAKES: 4 "sloppy Jenns"
TOTAL TIME: 10 minutes

Leftovers? This technique applies to all of the cooked meat mixes in this book.

The addition of mustard and brown sugar will revive and match the flavors in the already cooked meat.

1 tbsp (15 ml) butter

½ medium white onion, sliced

1 lb (0.5 kg) leftover cooked ground meat

½ tsp chili flakes

½ tsp dry mustard

1 tsp (6 g) brown sugar

4 English muffins

4 potato rolls, split

4 taco shells

4 large handfuls of corn chips

Melt the butter in a pan on medium heat. Add the onion once it's melted. Sauté for 3 minutes until it is translucent. Add the meat and spices. Break it up until it resembles a taco-meat mix. Since the meat is par cooked, it does not need to simmer long. If the spices are sticking to the pan, add a ¼ cup (60 ml) of water to scrape and incorporate. Cover for 5 minutes to avoid getting splatter on your stove.

Have it on an English muffin, on a potato roll, in a taco or on top of nachos (preferably Frito Pie style!).

BLACK BEAN BURGERS

MAKES: 8 burgers
TOTAL TIME: 45 minutes

I was paralyzed by the idea of grilling a substantial vegetarian option, let alone a vegan one. I faced a bit of criticism about a lack of diversity on my menus, so I was determined to give our veggie-eating friends more than just sides. All of my early tests for burgers were either crumbly or not holding together in a patty enough to put on a grill. The solution was to mash half the beans into a paste! These burgers freeze very well, so if you're not serving them all at once, wrap them individually in plastic wrap.

Nutritional yeast pulls double duty in helping thicken the burger mix and has a cheesy, fatty umami flavor that meat usually provides.

---

1 red onion, diced

Olive oil

2 cloves garlic

1 tsp (6 g) cumin

½ tsp salt

2 chopped chipotle peppers

3 cups (450 g) Cinnamon Black Beans (page 117)

½ tsp nutritional yeast

2 cups (118 g) panko bread crumbs

Sauté the onion on medium heat with a swirl of olive oil for 3 minutes until translucent and tender. Add the garlic and cook for another minute until it is fragrant. Add the cumin, salt and chipotle peppers and stir to incorporate.

Move these vegetables to the bowl of a food processor. Add half of the black beans and the nutritional yeast. Pulse into a paste and transfer it to a large bowl. Fold in the remaining black beans and 1 cup (59 g) of the bread crumbs. Put the other cup of bread crumbs in a shallow dish. Form 8 patties and coat each one in crumbs. Set each burger on a wire rack to dry out at room temperature for 30 minutes.

Technically, these burgers are ready to eat. But to serve hot, brush the grill with oil and cook for 3 to 4 minutes on each side until it is heated throughout.

PROJECT PARLOR
2012 SUMMER BBQ
COMPETITION
WINNER

ADOBO WANGS

MAKES: 8 to 10 chicken wings
TOTAL TIME: 2 hours and
25 minutes active, up to
12 hours passive

Traditionally, Filipino adobo is pieces of chicken simmered in a tangy gastrique of soy sauce and vinegar. I figured that since the soy sauce was salty, the cooking liquid could act as a brine.

1 cup (240 ml) white vinegar

1 cup (240 ml) soy sauce

1 head garlic, peeled

1 bay leaf

1 serrano chili pepper

2 lb (900 g) chicken wings

4 tbsp (60 ml) unsalted butter

4 tbsp (60 ml) bacon fat

Boil all of the ingredients together except for the chicken, butter and bacon fat. Bring it down to a simmer for 20 minutes to make a gastrique marinade. Add the chicken to the marinade and cook for 5 minutes. Turn the heat off and let it cool.

Move to the fridge and marinate for at least 4 hours, up to 12.

Prepare a smoker and hot smoke the wings for 2 hours until they reach an internal temperature of 175°F (80°C), 180°F (83°C) rested. As you wait, melt the butter and bacon fat in a saucepan. Whisk in a ¼ cup (60 ml) of the marinade and bring to a boil. Discard the rest of the marinade, it has raw chicken juice in it. Every 10 minutes, baste the wings with the butter-bacon marinade.

If you have a gas grill, cook the wings over direct heat for 2 minutes on each side, basting when you flip. Move the wings to indirect heat and cover with foil for an hour until the internal temperature reads 175°F (80°C).

PROJECT PARLOR
2012 SUMMER BBQ
COMPETITION
WINNER

BUTTERMILK CHICKEN SKEWERS

MAKES: 4 large or
8 small skewers
TOTAL TIME: 20 minutes
active, up to 8 hours passive

Milk is one of those things I keep buying at the store even when I already have a bottle at home. As a result, it spoils. This is totally okay! If you store it in a glass or plastic container, it is still usable as buttermilk. It should smell sour and have no other colors. Avoid any buttermilks or milks stored in cartons; the air exposure from the lip can promote mold growth, as I learned the hard way.

The softly textured chicken is the perfect vehicle for the garden-fresh herb butter with thyme, sage and oregano.

---

2 lb (900 g) chicken breast

2 cups (475 ml) buttermilk

¼ cup +1 tsp (75 g + 6 g) kosher salt

4 tbsp (40 g) fresh sage, chopped

2 tbsp (20 g) fresh thyme, stems removed

2 tbsp (20 g) oregano, chopped

¼ cup (60 ml) butter, melted

1 clove garlic, grated

2 tbsp (30 ml) olive oil

Soak wood skewers in cold water overnight.

Cut the chicken into 1-inch (25-mm) cubes and brine in the buttermilk and kosher salt for 4 to 8 hours.

Combine the herbs with the melted butter, garlic and olive oil. Store until you're ready to grill.

Skewer 3 pieces of chicken on each stick. Grill on each side for 6 to 7 minutes. Finish the skewers with a brush of melted herb butter. If you're doubling the recipe, a service trick I have is to keep the butter mixture in a grill-safe container on the cold side of the grill and dunk the sticks instead of brushing individually.

Alternatively, you can bake these skewers at 350°F (177°C) for 15 minutes, until they read an internal temperature of 165°F (74°C).

WHOLE LEMONGRASS CHICKEN

MAKES: 1 whole chicken platter for 2 to 4 people
TOTAL TIME: 1 hour active, up to 12 hours passive

Bashing lemongrass stalks is satisfying and therapeutic. How many dishes can you say that about? As part of our last hurrah and grab for the Project Parlor BBQ championship, we offered this chicken as an exclusive if you ordered our "Robert Baratheon's Feast" platter.

This method of splitting and grilling poultry is called spatchcocking. The secret to this epic bird is the Southeast Asian aromatics of lemongrass, ginger and garlic stuffed under the skin.

4 lb (1.8 kg) whole chicken

½ cup + 1 tsp (300 g + 6 g) kosher salt, divided

4 lemongrass stalks

2 cloves garlic, minced

1 thumb ginger, minced

Olive oil

Pepper

Brine the chicken overnight with ½ cup (300 g) of kosher salt and enough water to cover.

Cut the dry stalks of the lemongrass off. Discard the dirty outermost layer. Bash the juicy stalks in a mortar with a pestle or the blunt handle of a wooden spoon. Mix in the garlic and ginger and continue to mash it into a paste. Add 1 teaspoon (6 g) of salt and set the paste aside.

Drain the brine and pat the chicken dry. With the breast side down, cut through the backbone of the chicken. Flip it over and press down on the breast bone to break it. Save any innards (if they're still there) for another project. You should have a flattened chicken.

Run your fingers carefully under the chicken's skin. Spread the lemongrass paste under the chicken skin, as evenly as you can. Cover with plastic wrap and let rest in the fridge for at least 4 hours.

When you're ready to grill, brush the chicken with olive oil and sprinkle on a little more salt and freshly ground pepper. Cook the bird skin-side down over indirect heat for 25 minutes. Check the skin for burning, try not to fiddle with the chicken until you're ready to flip or you'll lose that skin to the grill.

Using two pairs of tongs or two large spatulas, flip the chicken and cook for 20 minutes before checking the temperature. It is done when it hits 165°F (74°C).

Serve hot on a cutting board with a knife through it. It's really dramatic just like *Game of Thrones*.

PROJECT PARLOR 2012 SUMMER BBQ COMPETITION WINNER

GRILLED STONE FRUIT

MAKES: 4 dessert servings
or 8 small bites

TOTAL TIME: 10 minutes

I love this dessert because it has no added sugar and the cheese works really well with caramelized fruit. The mint adds a freshness that pairs beautifully with stone fruit. Use blue cheeses like Gorgonzola, Caveman, Point Reyes or Buttermilk.

4 peaches, halved

4 plums, halved

2 tbsp (30 ml) olive oil

Salt

Pepper

1 cup (240 ml) plain yogurt

¼ cup (40 g) fresh mint, stems removed

¼ lb (113 g) blue cheese

Remove the pits from the fruit. Toss the fruit halves lightly with olive oil, a pinch of salt and 2 or 3 grinds of fresh pepper. Grill on the cut sides for 5 to 8 minutes until they soften and stick to the grill, remove with a spatula. If you try to use tongs, they will squish and bubble all over the place.

Flip and cover the fruit on the cold side of the grill with foil until you are ready to serve them.

Arrange 1 of each fruit half on a plate, dollop a spoonful of yogurt on top. Garnish with fresh mint, crumbled cheese, a grind of pepper and a couple drops of olive oil. Alternatively, you can pile everything together on one platter and have guests serve themselves.

Crowd Control

Competition isn't limited to adjudicated cook-offs. Many social situations will call upon your quick thinking improvisation skills as well as new-found preparedness. Brunch, holidays, parties, potlucks, unexpected guests and camping present their own unique challenges.

I will share how I prepare ahead as far as possible when cooking for groups. When I moved to Brooklyn, I had a tradition of serving grilled cheese at my house every Sunday. I hate eating the exact same thing twice, so I challenged myself to come up with a new cheese concoction every week. After a year and half of melty goodness, I decided to quit my music industry job and work at a restaurant. *Kitchen Confidential* in hand and an internship at Murray's Cheese launched me onto the professional (and winding) path I find myself on today.

LESSONS LEARNED

- Be conscious and plan how you will keep hot things hot and cold things cool.

- No platter? Use the cooking vessel. Make it easy for guests to serve themselves so you don't have to plate every single dish.

- Like in *The Simpsons*, have a "distraction plate" of scraps for anyone sneaking tastes in the kitchen. There is always someone you know that does this!

"FRIES"

MAKES: 1 pint (473 ml) pickles
TOTAL TIME: 10 minutes active, 2 days passive

During a "hold on to your buns" burger pop-up at Project Parlor, we thought it would be funny to ask people, "Would you like fries with that?" But instead of actual fries, it was a side of pickles that were shaped like fries. Was it a cruel joke? Probably. Daikon is a little funky but the peach is a fun, sweet foil to it.

1 cup (240 ml) water

2 tbsp (30 ml) honey

⅓ cup (80 ml) rice wine vinegar

1 tbsp (10 g) salt

½ tsp turmeric

¼ lb (113 g) daikon radish, cut into thick batons

1 firm peach, pitted and cut into batons

Combine the liquid ingredients in a small pot and bring to a boil. Turn off the heat and whisk in the salt and turmeric.

Prepare 2 clean and sanitized jars and place the daikon and peach batons in vertically. Pour the brine over the batons and let cool completely.

Cover the jars and store in the fridge for at least 2 days. The fries will keep for up to 2 weeks.

CINNAMON BLACK BEANS

MAKES: 4 cups (804 g)
vegan black beans
TOTAL TIME: 1 day

Jeff was a huge proponent of soaking our own beans and not buying canned (though it is totally acceptable). My issue was always time. I didn't have time to watch them simmer away on the stove. I grew to love my slow cooker, I could leave for work and have beans when I got home. This recipe is meant to be a base for other dishes. If you're going to have a side of beans for dinner, fold in a clove of grated garlic at the end and sprinkle on some queso fresco or, to keep it vegan, tofu sour cream.

16 oz (460 g) bag dry black beans

1 stick cinnamon

1 large white onion, sliced into rings

1 quart (950 ml) vegetable broth

1 tbsp (10 g) salt

1 clove garlic, grated, for serving, optional

Crumbled queso fresco, for serving, optional

Sour cream, for serving, optional

The night before you plan to serve the beans, wash the them and discard the water. Soak the beans overnight with enough cold water to cover them by 2 or 3 inches (5 to 8 cm). Discard the soaking liquid and place the black beans in a slow cooker with the cinnamon stick, onion, salt and vegetable broth. Cook on low for 6 to 8 hours until they are tender. The beans should not feel chalky in your mouth and should not have exploded. Discard the cinnamon stick before serving. Save the cooking liquid for rice or a soup.

PROJECT PARLOR
2012 SUMMER BBQ
COMPETITION
WINNER

HERB SLAW

MAKES: 4 cups (1.3 kg)
slaw or 8 side servings
TOTAL TIME: 45 minutes

I thought my sandwiches needed a good crunch, a burst of color and flavor. I remembered a Vietnamese herb salad I had once; the combination of mint and cilantro blew my mind. *Nuoc mam cham* is a very thin, fishy dressing. If you don't want to commit to two types of cabbage—honestly it's just for the showmanship of color—use one whole head of either green or purple, if you don't care what it looks like. Cabbage lasts longer than other salad greens at a BBQ, so it's been a staple on my menus for a long time. Alternatively, you can use the Miso Dressing on page 155.

½ head green cabbage

½ head purple cabbage

½ cup (75 g) cilantro

½ cup (75 g) mint

½ cup (75 g) dill

4 tsp (20 ml) Nuoc Mam Cham (page 155)

Remove any rubber bands or twine from the herbs and wash them by submerging them in cold water. Jostle them and drain, repeat two more times. You want to make sure you get any dirt out of the roots of where the stems were bunched together.

Chop the dirty root ends of the cilantro off and discard. Mince the stems and pluck the leaves off. Discard the hard stems of the mint and dill. Leave the mint leaves whole but run your knife through the dill once. Mix the herbs in a dry bowl and cover with a damp paper towel.

Discard the outermost leaves of the cabbage and rinse the whole head before slicing.

For a coarse, noodle-like slaw for sandwiches, slice the cabbage with a mandoline at ⅛-inch (3-mm) thickness.

For a minced, fast food–style slaw, run the cabbage through a food processor with the grater attachment. Note that it will produce some liquid that you will need to drain off and discard.

About 30 minutes before you plan to serve the slaw, toss the herbs, cabbage and Nuoc Mam Cham together. Store in the fridge to let the flavors meld. The slaw will reduce in volume. Taste and salt as desired.

PROJECT PARLOR
2012 SUMMER BBQ
COMPETITION
WINNER

POTATO SALAD WITH WASABI SESAME SEEDS

MAKES: 1 lb (453 g) potato salad, 4 side servings or 2 entrée servings

TOTAL TIME: 1 hour

I remember my shock and awe as I exclaimed, "EIGHT DOLLARS," at a bottle of wasabi sesame seeds in the store. The pop of crunchy seeds and a kick of nose-flaring wasabi sounded like a good idea. My potato salad recipe at the time was pretty boring and lacked color. The solution to doing this at home was simply toasting the seeds to release their oils, readying them for a bath of wasabi.

1 lb (0.5 kg) Yukon Gold potatoes, washed

1 tsp (6 g) salt, plus a few more pinches

1 tbsp (10 g) sesame seeds

1 tsp (6 g) wasabi powder

1 clove garlic, peeled

4 tbsp (60 ml) Meyer Lemon Mayo (page 153)

4 scallions, chopped into rings

Pepper

Cube the potatoes into 1-inch (25-mm) pieces and place in a pot, cover with cold water. Throw in a generous pinch of salt. Bring the pot to a boil and lower to a simmer for 8 to 12 minutes, until the potatoes are fork tender. Drain and let the potatoes cool.

Toast the sesame seeds over medium heat for 2 minutes until they start to brown. You should be able to smell them. Off the heat, put them in a jar with the wasabi powder. Put on the lid and shake it like the dickens. Pop off the lid to let the mix completely cool.

Meanwhile, grate the garlic into a medium bowl with a microplane. Combine with the mayo, scallion and few grinds of coarse pepper. Once the potatoes are cool, toss them in the mayo mixture. Chill for 30 minutes or more. When you are ready to serve, garnish with the wasabi sesame seeds.

If you are eating this in the winter, eat the potatoes warm and skip the last step of chilling.

PROJECT PARLOR 2012 SUMMER BBQ COMPETITION WINNER

BITTERS MELON SALAD

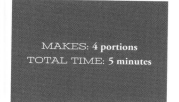

MAKES: **4 portions**
TOTAL TIME: **5 minutes**

When you think of melon, you may think of just watermelon, cantaloupe or honeydew. There are over 20 varieties. Canary melon looks like a yellow football with sweet flesh that has its own unique, perfume-y character.

This salad is a play on another piece of produce, the bitter melon or *ampalaya* in the Philippines. It appears in savory stews, flavored with shrimp paste. It is far too bitter for my delicate American palate, but the idea of bitter fruit is one to be explored for sure.

½ canary melon, peeled and cubed

¼ cup (60 ml) Dandelion Pesto (page 156)

½ cup (75 g) grape tomato, halved lengthwise

4–8 drops bitters

Tomato Salt (page 158)

Toss the melon cubes with the dandelion pesto in a mixing bowl. Divide and spoon them onto four small plates. Garnish each salad with tomatoes. Add 1 or 2 drops of bitters to each salad, aim for the open cut side of a tomato. Finish with a pinch of Tomato Salt before serving.

CHOPPED CHICKPEA SANDWICH

MAKES: 4 sandwiches
TOTAL TIME: 45 minutes

One of my first random sandwich deliveries was to a band called Lymbyc Systym. Before I opened my service up to the public, I was messaging bands on Myspace and asking if they needed fresh food delivered to their gigs. I knew the touring life was a disaster of quick service Mexican food and gas station snacks. Little did I know that this delivery would be a challenge! Jared Bell was vegan, and I wasn't familiar with the practice yet. I needed to come up with a sandwich without cheese but still substantial to someone who has been traveling a lot.

I looked to chickpeas because hummus is a common rider request from bands to eat backstage. It was sort of my nod to the music industry. I had a great time at the show and delivered my sandwiches backstage at the old Knitting Factory. Note that you can substitute the sweet pepper with bell or jarred piquillo. Now that I think about it, I should have used the bell peppers for the Bell brothers.

---

16 oz (460 g) cooked chickpeas

1 small cucumber, chopped

¼ cup (105 g) chopped sweet pepper

1 tbsp (15 ml) white wine vinegar

2 tbsp (30 ml) olive oil

1 clove garlic, minced

Salt and pepper to taste

4 seeded sub rolls

¼ cup (60 ml) Vegan Whipped Cheese (page 169)

2 tbsp (20 g) fresh parsley, chopped

Roughly chop the chickpeas and mix in the cucumber, sweet pepper, vinegar, olive oil and garlic. Add salt and pepper to your liking. Store in the fridge for 30 minutes to let the flavors develop.

Split the rolls in half, leaving a hinge on one side. Scoop out the soft insides of the bread to make a trough. Toast the inside of the bread face down in an unoiled pan or face up in the broiler for 2 minutes. Spread the vegan cheese on the top half of the roll and fill the sandwich with chickpea salad and finish each with fresh parsley.

Alternatively, you can serve the chopped chickpea mixture as a side salad on its own.

¡WATERMELON!

MAKES: 10 to 12 slices of boozy melon
TOTAL TIME: 40 minutes

Watermelon is excellent company to a cookout. In our preparation for competition, however, we were disappointed that the watermelon didn't last too long if we soaked it in tequila and honey beforehand. It was mushy, and the cell walls broke down too much. I saw Jeff spritzing his house plants one day, and it hit me: we should spray it on before serving! Honey dissolves quickly in the hot water, so be sure to chill the mixture before spraying on the melon.

2½ lb (1125 g) watermelon

2 tbsp (30 ml) honey

¼ cup (60 ml) hot water

2 to 4 ice cubes

2 oz (60 ml) tequila

1 tsp (6 g) salt

Pepper

1 cup (240 ml) plain yogurt

¼ cup (60 ml) fresh mint leaves

Slice the watermelon into 1-inch (25-mm) wedges and set aside in the fridge.

Dissolve the honey in the hot water and then add the ice cubes to cool it down. Add the tequila and transfer to a food-safe spray bottle. Chill for 30 minutes in the fridge.

While you wait, add the salt and a few grinds of coarse pepper to the yogurt. Remove the stems from the mint leaves.

To assemble, spray the watermelon on both sides with the honey tequila. Top with a dollop of savory yogurt and a few mint leaves.

PROJECT PARLOR
2012 SUMMER BBQ
COMPETITION
WINNER

SPICED HAM BUTTER

MAKES: **1 cup (230 g)**
compound butter

TOTAL TIME: **5 minutes**
active, **2 hours** passive

I remember ordering French radishes with toast at a restaurant and exclaiming, "That's it? This dish is seven dollars?" It was simply the radishes, crusty bread, butter and chunky sea salt. The radishes were long and not fat like I had seen in the stores. I pursed my lips and prepared myself a piece of toast. What happened next was a remarkable and oddly satisfying, crisp texture. I ate this for breakfast at home for at least the two weeks following that moment.

One Thanksgiving, I bought a ham roast thinking that we didn't have enough food for guests. It ended up being way too much! I had to think of a way to preserve the ham without taking too much room in the fridge. Why not a compound butter?

½ cup (75 g) cooked ham roast, cubed

Orange zest

¼ tsp ground cloves

1 cup (230 g) unsalted butter, room temperature

1 loaf crusty French bread, for serving

1 bunch French radishes, for serving

Sea salt, for serving

Prepare a long piece of plastic wrap or parchment paper on a flat surface.

If you're using an immersion blender, place the ham in a tall jar.

If you're using a food processor, put it in the bowl. Pulse the ham until it forms small crumbles, then add the orange zest and clove. Combine with the butter and mix on low until the butter is pervasively pink and fluffy.

Using a spatula, transfer the butter to a sheet of parchment paper. Roll into a log shape, twist the ends and tie closed with twine. Chill for at least 2 hours before serving. If you will be freezing it, wrap plastic around the parchment log tightly.

Best experienced with a slice of crusty bread, French radishes and chunky sea salt. If not, any unsalted situation would lovingly play well with ham butter.

WILD MUSHROOMS

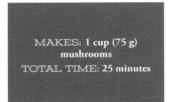

MAKES: 1 cup (75 g)
mushrooms
TOTAL TIME: 25 minutes

I wasn't in love with mushrooms growing up. They were slimy and turned this ugly brown when they sat out on the crudités plate at parties. I picked them off of my pizza slices and quietly slid them out of my salads with a fork. It wasn't until I was prepping brunch at Home/Made that I discovered the perfume of mushrooms that weren't white buttons. Cremini, shiitake and oyster had luxurious textures and meaty smells. Use this mix on omelets, sandwiches or even as a side dish to a steak. I like to use a mix of shiitake, mature pink oyster mushrooms and maitake. You can use any varieties as long as they are fresh and from a trusted source.

---

20 oz (550 g) wild mushrooms

1 tsp (5 ml) white miso paste

½ cup (120 ml) dregs of light beer, white wine, sake or water

2 tbsp (30 ml) butter

1 shallot, minced

1 clove garlic, grated

Salt and pepper to taste

Brush off any dirt from the mushrooms, use a paper towel or dry brush to give them a quick wipe. Cut off the dirty "foot" or where the mushroom had made contact with the ground or tree. Try to keep as much of the stem as possible. Slice the mushrooms into ¼-inch (6-mm) pieces. If you're working with maitake, break the bouquets with your hands into branches where their stems are ¼ inch (6 mm) in width.

Place the mushrooms in a pan on medium heat to dry them out for 7 to 10 minutes. Meanwhile, whisk the miso with your choice of liquid and set aside.

As the mushrooms release water, add the butter and shallot. After 2 minutes and once the shallot is translucent, add the garlic. If the mushrooms aren't sizzling and look too dry, add a swirl of olive oil. Sauté for 5 minutes. Turn the heat all the way up and deglaze the mushrooms with the miso liquid. Reduce for 4 to 5 minutes on low heat until it forms a thick sauce. Turn off the heat and let rest in the pan for 5 minutes. Taste and salt it as needed.

MUSHROOM HOAGIE

MAKES: 1 yummy
vegetarian sandwich
TOTAL TIME: 25 minutes

Even a huge meathead like me loves this sub sando. My mushroom mix's miso-umami goes really well with aged Swiss cheeses like Appenzeller, Emmentaler, Raclette, Hoch Ybrig (and pretty much any cheese aged by Rolf Beeler). Other alternatives are Pleasant Ridge Reserve and L'Etivaz. I like to get bread from Philadelphia when I visit, but if you can't find one, a long sub roll will work.

½ white onion, sliced thinly into rings

1 tbsp (15 g) butter, sliced in 2

¼ cup (60 ml) water

¼ tsp ancho powder

1 hoagie roll

⅛ lb (55 g) Swiss cheese, sliced thinly

1 handful arugula, washed

½ tsp lemon juice

Salt and pepper

⅓ cup (50 g) Wild Mushrooms (page 128)

Preheat your broiler on high.

Sauté the onions on medium heat with half of the butter. When they are translucent, pour on the water and simmer for 10 minutes. Continue to cook on low heat for 8 to 10 more minutes until they are browned. Stir in the ancho powder. Let cool and set aside.

Split the hoagie roll and spread the butter on the insides. Layer the cheese on both sides and broil on a baking sheet for 2 minutes until the cheese starts to bubble. Turn off the oven and move the bread to the top-most rack.

Toss the arugula in the lemon juice quickly with a pinch of salt and a turn of fresh pepper.

Assemble the hoagie with the hot cheese roll, arugula on one side, then hot mushroom mix and onion on the other side. Devour!

HEN OF THE WOODS BOUQUETS

MAKES: 10 to 12 bouquets
TOTAL TIME: 20 minutes

Hen of the Woods, or maitake mushrooms, are showstoppers. Use these bouquets as a garnish to ramen, rice bowls, salad or as a whimsical amuse bouche snack. If you can't find these mushrooms, try enoki.

Fragrant mushroom and toasty seaweed work together in an unexpected but complementary way.

1 lb (0.5 kg) Hen of the Woods mushrooms, heads intact

1 package toasted seaweed sheets

1 tbsp (15 g) butter

Kosher salt

Cut off the dirt "foot" at the base of the mushrooms.

Brush the head lightly to clean any visible dirt with a wet paper towel or food-safe brush.

Starting from the stipe (the solid white flesh at the bottom), separate the mushrooms into 1½-inch- (4-cm-) wide florets, like you would with broccoli.

Prepare a cast-iron pan on high heat.

Cut as many 1-inch- (25-mm-) wide seaweed strips as you have mushroom florets.

Sear the mushrooms for 2 minutes on each side, remove from the heat and let cool.

Wrap each mushroom's base with seaweed and seal with a dab of water.

Reduce the cast iron's heat to medium. Place your mushroom bouquets in the pan, seaweed seam–side down. Weigh them down with a cast-iron press or the bottom of another clean cast-iron pan.

Press for 3 minutes and check that the mushrooms are releasing water. If they are, flip each mushroom and add the butter to the pan. Tilt it to coat. Season with a pinch of kosher salt. Replace the press and cook for another 3 minutes.

Do not fiddle or flip the mushrooms again; you want them to dry up but soak up the butter. They should be standing up straight and not floppy. If the seaweed starts to burn, reduce the heat and wait a couple more minutes for the mushroom to lose moisture.

WONTON FRUIT CUP

MAKES: 8 small fruit cups
TOTAL TIME: 15 minutes

The fruit cup was another attempt as reducing the amount of cutlery we had to buy for Project Parlor. It's a little messy, but essentially we made the fruit salad container edible! Tart grapes and sweet, succulent peaches marry well with the salinity of blue cheese. If you can't find Caveman blue cheese, a gorgonzola would be an excellent replacement.

Ingredients	Instructions
16 square wonton wrappers	Preheat the oven to 350°F (177°C).
Vegetable oil	Brush both sides of each wonton with vegetable oil before placing 8 in a muffin tin. Layer another wonton on top of each cup but rotate them 90° so there are four corners sticking up. Use your fingers to push the wontons down into the cups as far as they can go. Bake for 5 to 10 minutes until they are crispy and brown. No part of the cups should be pliable or stark white.

16 square wonton wrappers

Vegetable oil

¼ lb (113 g) Caveman blue cheese

1 cup (240 ml) heavy cream

1 cup (150 g) seedless green grapes

2 peaches, pitted and cubed

1 pear, cored and cubed

1 lemon, juiced and zested

Pepper

Preheat the oven to 350°F (177°C).

Brush both sides of each wonton with vegetable oil before placing 8 in a muffin tin. Layer another wonton on top of each cup but rotate them 90° so there are four corners sticking up. Use your fingers to push the wontons down into the cups as far as they can go. Bake for 5 to 10 minutes until they are crispy and brown. No part of the cups should be pliable or stark white.

Turn off the oven and let them continue to cook if they need a little more time. Pull them out of the tin and drain on paper towels to cool.

In a mixing bowl, mash the cheese and heavy cream together. Whip it with an immersion blender if you want a smooth sauce, but I prefer it chunky. Fold in the cut fruit and lemon juice. Scoop salad into the wonton cups and finish with a bit of lemon zest and freshly ground pepper.

If you are not serving right away, put the salad in the cups at the very last moment possible, or they will wilt.

LUMPIA CHIPS

MAKES: 150 triple layer chips
TOTAL TIME: 15 minutes

Lumpia is a thin egg roll sheet available in many specialty grocery stores. You'll find it in the freezer section. Besides making Filipino egg rolls (roll up any stir fry and seal with egg!), I like to make chips for nachos. Note that as you work with lumpia sheets, they dry out quickly, so keep a damp paper towel over the stack as you work. If you can't find lumpia sheet, you can use wonton wrappers, but skip the folding step because they are thicker.

1 (25-count) pack lumpia egg roll sheets

½ cup (120 ml) vegetable oil

Preheat the oven to 350°F (177°C).

Fold each sheet into thirds, like a letter in a long envelope. With kitchen-safe scissors or a chef's knife, cut each folded sheet into 6 strips. You should have 6 triple layer pieces; keep them folded.

Oil a baking sheet and place the chips down in a single layer. Brush the tops with more vegetable oil, making sure it soaks through the 3 layers of each chip. Bake for 5 to 10 minutes. The chips should be a light toasted brown and crisp, not pale white or pliable.

Drain on paper towels and let cool completely before storing in an airtight container. No need to refrigerate.

1ST PLACE, PEOPLE'S CHOICE 2011 BACON TAKEDOWN

MISO GRITTY

MAKES: 4 large cakes or
8 snack sizes

TOTAL TIME: 2 hours,
30 minutes

The Grits Takedown is one that lives in infamy. Not because of who won or lost, but because of the venue. It took place during the Food Film Festival, and 20 cooks were invited to the old tobacco warehouse in DUMBO to compete. This was my first time cooking with grits *and* cooking onsite. Usually we had sterno heaters and pans, but I wanted to fry my grit cakes à la minute. Because I required electricity in this very rustic venue, I was placed next to Nicole Taylor, who was cooking her grits on the fly. It was blazing hot outside, and the warehouse was known for not having a roof or running water. We had to run across a bike path to the park to use the hose. Nevertheless, many of us competitors bonded over the experience.

Buttery grits are pumped up with miso and scallion and cooled into slicable cakes that are later fried in bacon fat.

---

1 quart (950 ml) half and half

1 tbsp (15 ml) white miso

1 cup (150 g) coarse grits

1 stick butter, cubed

Salt

6 scallions, chopped into rings

1 tsp (6 g) white pepper

¼ cup (60 ml) bacon fat

2 tbsp (20 g) pickled ginger, chopped

Bring the half and half to a boil in a pot. Lower the heat to a simmer. Add the miso and prepare to whisk. Slowly add the grits as you keep whisking and then throw in a cube of butter, gradually over the course of 15 minutes. The grits are done when they don't crunch in your mouth. They should have absorbed the liquid and have a creamy mouthfeel. Taste and salt them as needed.

Let the grits cool for 10 minutes. While they are still warm, fold in ½ the amount of scallion and all of the white pepper. Transfer the grits to a baking sheet lined with parchment paper. Tap the pan on the counter to even out the grits and release any air pockets. Cover the pan with plastic wrap and chill for 2 hours, until the grits are solid. If they are still goopy, continue to chill.

Remove the plastic wrap and flip the giant grit cake onto a cutting board. Take off the parchment paper. Cut the grits into 4 pieces (or more if you want). Melt the bacon fat in a frying pan and fry the cakes on medium heat until they crisp up on the edges, 5 minutes. Flip and cook for another 5 minutes.

Drain the cakes lightly on a paper towel and top with the pickled ginger and remaining scallions.

LOB GNARLEYS

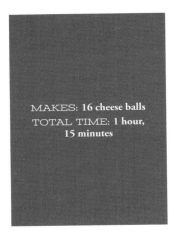

MAKES: **16 cheese balls**
TOTAL TIME: **1 hour,
15 minutes**

Seafood was foreign to me until I was 27 years old. At sushi places, I'd quietly order the cucumber rolls or avocado. My father used to eat stinky kipper snacks with rice, and I'd try not to gag on my toaster pastry. I've since completely come around to fish, but shellfish was another story. I'm not sure if it was the shock of killing Sebastian from *The Little Mermaid*, but I've always had a hard time with it. Even when we had a lobster special at Home/Made, we made Jeff put the lobsters in the water and crack them later. We could hear them scratching at the sides of the pot—oh God!

Fast forward to the Lobster Takedown supply pick-up. I was staring down 10 pounds (4.5 kg) of lobster claw and tail in a Styrofoam container. What was an unexpected way to present an ingredient that was having a moment on buttered split-top buns? I got stuck on the idea of incorporating cheese, because cheese and seafood don't usually show up together on menus. It was worth the risk because this dish won judge's Honorable Mention. Lob Gnarleys are smoky, crunchy cheese balls that are ready to party . . . or chill, whatever.

Maplewood chips

16 oz (450 g) goat cheese

1 cup (150 g) roasted almonds

1 lb (0.5 kg) cooked lobster meat, divided

2 cloves garlic, minced

Salt

1 tsp (6 g) ancho pepper powder

1 tbsp (10 g) onion powder

Soak the wood chips overnight.

When you're ready, prepare a smoker with the maple chips. Smoke the goat cheese on a sheet pan, making sure not to apply direct heat to the cheese. The cheese is done when it turns a light brown on the outside, approximately 30 minutes. It is okay if it melts a little.

Chop the almonds and set them aside. Mince ¼ cup (55 g) of the lobster, then pull the rest into ½-inch (13-mm) pieces. When the cheese is done smoking, let it cool completely. Fold in the garlic, minced lobster, salt and ancho pepper.

To assemble, form 16 cheese balls. Dust the larger pieces of lobster with onion powder and push a chunk into the middle of each ball. Roll it between your hands to seal it and then roll it in the almonds. Chill for 30 minutes before serving.

If you do not have a smoker, add 1 teaspoon (5 ml) of liquid smoke to the goat cheese when combining all of the ingredients.

JUDGE'S
HONORABLE MENTION
2015 LOBSTER
TAKEDOWN
BROOKLYN

DEVILISH OLD BAE

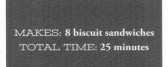

MAKES: 8 biscuit sandwiches
TOTAL TIME: 25 minutes

I had a lot of leftover Luke's Lobster from the Takedown. Naturally I wanted to make sandwiches. I imagine this is what people in the Hamptons have all the time, because lobster just grows on trees over there.

This is a mashup of deviled eggs and egg salad. Rich soft-cooked yolk blankets fresh lobster on a cheesy biscuit bun.

2 cups (440 g) self-rising flour

2 tbsp (30 g) cocktail sauce seasoning (such as Old Bay), divided

½ tsp cayenne pepper

1 cup (240 ml) heavy cream

½ cup (45 g) cheddar, grated

2 tbsp (30 ml) butter, melted

6 eggs

1 tbsp (15 ml) Dijon mustard

1 tbsp (10 g) chives, chopped finely

1 lb (0.5 kg) fresh lobster meat, cubed

Preheat the oven to 425°F (218°C).

Mix the flour, 1 tablespoon (15 g) of Old Bay, cayenne pepper and heavy cream together to form a sticky dough. Fold in the cheddar. Form 8 large biscuits and set them on a greased baking sheet. Cook the biscuits for 10 to 15 minutes, until their bottoms are toasty brown. Brush them with butter and sprinkle on the remaining Old Bay.

Boil a small pot of water. Add the eggs carefully and cook for 4 minutes and 30 seconds. Prepare an ice bath and shock the eggs until they are completely cool. Peel the eggs and separate the yolks (use the whites for a breakfast sandwich or something). Whisk the egg yolks with the mustard and chive. Toss the lobster in the sauce.

Split an old bae biscuit in half and add a hefty spoonful of dressed lobster. Adjust your monocle.

WHAM BAM THANK YOU LAMB!

I was listening to a lot of Bowie as I was preparing for the Lamb Takedown. We had a choice of different cuts of meat, and I chose the shank because it was the most unfamiliar. Who does that going into competition? Shouldn't I have been going with what I knew? Well, that is not how I operate.

Shank requires a long period of braising. I thought back to Filipino parties when I was growing up. We would have these gigantic pig roasts at every major occasion. The interesting part is leftovers of that roast or even turkey from Thanksgiving was turned into *paksiw*, a stew of the shredded meat with *mang tomas* sauce. What I thought was simple gravy turned out to be liver, brown sugar, bread crumbs and lots of black pepper. The sugar does a great job of masking the mineral flavor of the liver.

At the competition, I served the braised lamb "nacho style" on my own Lumpia Chips (page 134). Here, enjoy the lamb over rice or in a slider sandwich.

MAKES: 4 servings
TOTAL TIME: 2 hours, 35 minutes

---

1 pint (500 g) chicken liver

1 cup (240 ml) milk

Butter

1 medium red onion, chopped

½ cup (90 g) brown sugar

½ cup (30 g) butter cracker crumbs

A dash apple brandy

Vinegar

4 lamb shanks

Salt and pepper, to taste

2 cups (475 ml) dry white wine

4 cloves garlic, sliced

2 cups (475 ml) unsalted chicken broth

4 slide buns, for serving

4 servings of cooked white rice, for serving

For the mang tomas, wash the liver in cold water and drain. Soak them in the milk for 20 minutes and up to an hour. Drain and discard the milk.

Meanwhile, melt the butter in a pan and sauté the onion for 3 minutes until it is translucent and softens. Add the liver and cook for 3 minutes on each side. Transfer onions to the bowl of a food processor and add the liver, brown sugar, crumbs, apple brandy and vinegar. Blend until everything is broken down; it will look very brown and won't be completely smooth. Store in an airtight container until ready to use.

For the shanks, preheat the oven to 350°F (177°C).

Salt and pepper the lamb shanks and set aside. In a roasting pan with a lid, stir the mang tomas with the white wine, garlic and chicken broth. Place the lamb shanks in a single layer in the sauce and cover.

Bake for 2 hours, covered until the meat is tender and easily falls off the bone.

Remove the shanks to a plate to cool. With a butter knife, scoop out the shank's bone marrow. Whisk it into the pan sauce. Pull the meat off the shanks and fold into the sauce. If you are eating soon, turn off the oven, cover the pan again and hold the lamb there until you are ready to eat.

3RD PLACE. 2010 BROOKLYN LAMB TAKEDOWN

Grand Finale Finishers

Imagine that booming voice from Mortal Kombat, "FINISH HIM!" Akin to the famous video game moment, a textural crunch, delightful pop or silky sauce can add that extra kick a dish needs. Whenever I'd be developing a new recipe, there would be something missing. Jeff would smack his lips and suggest more lemon. He always said that! In spite, I spent many nights poring over his copy of the *Flavor Bible* (Page, Dorneburg, 2008) to figure out what else we could sprinkle, squeeze or spray onto our dishes.

LESSONS LEARNED

- Consider the timing of when your food is served. Will you premix it, or will that hurt the quality of the dish?

- Think about how you will store your condiments during service. Does it need to be on ice, or can it be at room temperature for a while?

- Hit your hot dishes with crunchy and saucy garnishes at the last possible moment, or they will wilt and lose their appeal.

All of these finishers accomplish something for my dishes:

BRIGHTNESS: Usually consisting of citrus, these balance salt and bitter flavors.

TEXTURE: I just love a crunchy thing. Love it. Any opportunity I can take to crumble bacon, pork rinds or fried shallots on anything, I'll do it, if it makes sense.

CONTRAST: I play with a lot of contrasting colors because some scientists argue that digestion begins when you see food and start to salivate. Color isn't the most important thing in a dish, but it does make me explore new ingredients that can accomplish both flavor and visual appeal.

SALINITY: Some of my recipes are under-seasoned because I consider the cumulative effect of its condiment.

LUBRICATION: Dry bread with proteins always needs some kind of lubrication from fat or cheese. The roof of your mouth will thank you.

Killer garnishes help balance and should not overwhelm your dish. My goal is to make them exciting enough that they are a talking point or possible springboard for another dish.

ADVIEH SPICE MIX

MAKES: ½ cup (47 g) spice mix
TOTAL TIME: 5 minutes

Advieh is an ancient Mesopotamian spice mix. It is warm and comforting with a floral nose on account of the rose and cardamom. Try a little in a milky tea, white meat mixes or sauces.

3 tsp (16 g) cumin seeds
5 tsp (28 g) cardamom pods
4 tsp (22 g) ground cinnamon
4 tsp (22 g) ground nutmeg
5 tsp (28 g) rose petals

Toast the cumin seeds and cardamom pods in a dry pan for 1 to 2 minutes and let them cool completely. Using a coffee grinder, pulse the seeds and pods into a powder. Combine the rest of the ingredients in a bowl. Store in an airtight container.

CHICKEN DUST

MAKES: 1½ cups (142 g) chicken dust
TOTAL TIME: 50 minutes

No lie, when you make this garnish, it looks straight up illegal. Easily alarm your family and friends by generously sprinkling what looks like a lot of marijuana on soups, rice or fried eggs.

Chicken dust is pulverized chicken dried with a mix of lemon, vinegar, soy sauce and brown sugar.

1 cup (150 g) cooked chicken, deboned
¼ cup (60 ml) soy sauce
¼ cup (60 ml) vinegar
2 tbsp (23 g) brown sugar
1 tbsp (10 g) lemon zest
½ cup (75 g) chives, chopped roughly

Set your broiler to high.

Pull the chicken apart roughly with your fingers and then use two forks to pull it into threads. Toss the meat with the soy sauce, vinegar and brown sugar. Broil for 7 to 10 minutes until the liquid has evaporated. Let the pan cool, reduce the oven to 200°F (93°C).

Combine the chicken, lemon zest and chives in the bowl of a food processor. Pulse 2 or 3 times before turning the machine completely on. The chicken should turn a bright green hue and start clumping together. Put the mix back into a baking sheet and spread it evenly.

Dry the chicken in the oven for 30 minutes at 200°F (93°C) until the dust has lost all moisture. Let cool again before storing in an airtight container.

For an "extra-green" appearance, the mix will be a little wet but skip the last 30 minutes of drying.

MISO PESTO

MAKES: 1 cup (240 ml) pesto
TOTAL TIME: 5 minutes

Toasted walnuts give new life to the idea of pesto. I've found that they are more cost effective and last longer than the traditional pine nuts. My pesto is meant to accompany the "I Like It Shallot" Burger (page 100), but do not feel limited to that singular use. Toss it with pasta, smear it on sandwiches or use as an easy salad dressing by adding a squeeze of lemon and more olive oil.

1 tbsp (15 ml) white miso

1 clove garlic

½ cup (75 g) walnuts, toasted

1 bunch basil, washed

½ cup plus 2 tbsp (120 ml plus 30 ml) olive oil, divided

Salt

Lemon juice, optional

Place the miso, garlic, walnuts and basil in the bowl of a food processor. Pulse until you've broken up the miso and the majority of the leaves.

Leave the processor running on low and slowly add the olive oil in a steady stream. Once you've finished, stop the blades and scrape the sides of the bowl down with a spatula.

When the pesto is smooth, taste and salt it as needed. Transfer to a plastic container and finish with the remaining olive oil before slapping the lid on that sucker, though I guarantee it won't last long.

ANCHO ACHUETE OIL

MAKES: 1 cup (240 ml) infused oil
TOTAL TIME: 30 minutes

Achuete is a bright red oil infused with annatto seeds, garlic, bay leaves, peppercorns and chili peppers. Annatto is what gives chorizo its vibrant red as well as the orange of American cheese. Annatto seeds can be found in the spice aisle or on Latin American ingredient shelves. Besides color, I wanted another way to use up my cache of dried chili peppers.

2 dried ancho chiles

1 cup (240 ml) water

2 garlic cloves, smashed

1 tsp (6 g) coriander seeds

1 tsp (6 g) peppercorns

1 cup (240 ml) vegetable oil

1 tbsp (10 g) annatto seeds

Break off the stems from the ancho peppers. Boil the water and soak the chilis for 15 to 20 minutes, until they are soft. Drain the water (or use it for broth!) and dry the pepper shards with a paper towel. Slice the peppers into ¼-inch (6-mm) strings and combine with the garlic, coriander and peppercorns in a jar.

Heat the vegetable oil and annatto seeds in a small pan until they barely start to bubble around the edges. Turn off the heat and let it infuse for 5 minutes. Strain the oil and add it to the jar with the rest of the ingredients. Let the oil completely cool before covering and placing in the fridge.

WHOLE GRAIN MUSTARD

MAKES: 1½ cups (355 ml)
mustard
TOTAL TIME: 1 hour,
15 minutes

I learned the beginnings of my mustard recipe from Alton Brown. I like an equal mix of brown and yellow mustard seed, but if you want to keep to one color, I completely understand! Yellow seeds are larger and have more of a "pop" than their dark counterparts. If you don't like whole grains, you can blend the mustard after it cools, be careful not to breathe in directly over the mixture. As Brown warns, do not combine ground mustard with water without heating it in the microwave or stovetop; it will make mustard gas!

½ cup (70 g) mustard seeds

½ cup (120 ml) spicy pickle juice

¼ cup (60 ml) stale beer

½ cup (120 ml) rice wine vinegar

2 tsp (11 g) dark brown sugar

1 tsp (6 g) kosher salt

¼ tsp hot paprika

1 clove garlic, grated

Place the mustard seeds in a jar.

Combine the liquids in a small pot and bring to boil. Turn off the heat and whisk in the sugar, salt, paprika and garlic. Pour the brine into the jar with the seeds. Stir to combine.

Let it cool completely before covering with a lid. Let the mustard cure for at least 2 days in the fridge before trying it. It will thicken over time as the seeds absorb the brine.

PICKLED CHIVE BUDS

MAKES: 1 pint (473 g) pickles
TOTAL TIME: 5 minutes active, up to 1 week passive

Something I like to do is to walk down every aisle of a grocery store or specialty market. Scanning shelves this way allows me to discover ingredients I probably never would have encountered if I just went to the store to grab specific things from a list every time. At the Hong Kong Supermarket in Manhattan, I discovered bouquets of chive flowers. These nascent buds are thicker than chives and are a little like ramps. Since each bundle comes with so many, I could only think to pickle them to keep them longer! It turns out that their stalks are the perfect length for a sandwich.

Fun fact: If you cut off the ends and store the chives in water, the flowers will bloom into these purple puffs that you can use as a garnish.

---

1 bunch chive stems, buds intact

1 cup (240 ml) vinegar

1 tbsp (15 ml) honey

1 tsp (6 g) peppercorns

Steam and sanitize a tall jar and its lid. Place the cleaned chive stems into the jar, cut from the green bottoms if they don't fit with the lid screwed on. Bring the vinegar to a boil in a small pot. Turn off the heat and whisk in the honey. Pour the brine and the peppercorns into the jar. Fill the remaining space with ice and let it melt. Top it off with cold water and store in the fridge overnight. The pickles will reach equilibrium after a week.

PROJECT PARLOR
2012 SUMMER BBQ
COMPETITION
WINNER

MUSTARD CRÈME

MAKES: 1 cup (240 ml)
decadent mustard crème
TOTAL TIME: 5 minutes

One of my favorite Escoffier recipes is *sauce moutarde à la crème*, which is essentially the addition of heavy cream and a few drops of lemon juice to prepared mustard. You can try this, but instead of cream, why not straight up cheese? If you can't find St. André, try Brillat Savarin, Explorateur, Pierre Robert or any triple crème cheese.

½ cup (120 ml) **Whole Grain Mustard (page 146)**

⅛ lb (55 g) **triple crème cheese (such as St. André)**

Half and half, if needed

Toasted baguette points

Blend the mustard and cheese in a food processor or in a medium mixing bowl with an immersion blender. A really ripe triple crème cheese will be a little weepy and melty from all the fat in it. If you have trouble blending it with the mustard into a smooth sauce, add a splash of half and half until it is spoonable. Store in an airtight container for up to one week and serve on toasted baguette points.

CHERMOULA

MAKES: 1½ cups (368 g) sauce
TOTAL TIME: 10 minutes

When you make Herb Slaw (page 118) and have leftover herbs, you can use them to make this bright green sauce that is perfect to brush on grilled breads, fish and chicken.

1 jalapeño, stemmed and seeded

1 cup (240 ml) extra virgin olive oil, divided

½ cup (80 g) Italian parsley leaves

½ cup (80 g) fresh cilantro leaves

½ cup (80 g) fresh mint leaves

½ cup (80 g) dill, stems removed

1 lemon, juiced and zest reserved

1 thumb ginger, peeled and chopped

½ tsp espelette pepper

Kosher salt

Combine all of the ingredients except olive oil and salt in the bowl of a food processor and pulse a few times to loosen it up. Add ½ cup (118 ml) of the olive oil and blend on low until combined. Scrape down the sides if there are still large pieces.

Using a spatula, transfer the coarse herbs to a container and pour the remaining oil on top. Stir and season with salt to your liking.

To store, cover and keep in the fridge for up to a week. The mix will separate over time, simply bring to room temperature and stir again.

PROJECT PARLOR
2012 SUMMER BBQ
COMPETITION
WINNER

CHER-MEOW-LA

MAKES: 2 cups (473 ml)
creamy sauce
TOTAL TIME: 5 minutes

I had the most amazing cilantro sour cream from Gato in Atlanta, Georgia. This is a tribute to that sauce that utilizes the stems of the cilantro.

1 cup (240 ml) Chermoula (page 157)

1 cup (240 ml) sour cream

Splash of white vinegar

Make the chermoula as directed but add the cilantro stems, making sure to discard the dirty root ends. Fold the chermoula into the sour cream and vinegar. Chill until ready to serve.

KIMCHI APPLES

MAKES: 1 quart (946 g)
kimchi apples
TOTAL TIME: 10 minutes
active, up to 3 weeks passive

The idea that grated Asian pear is used in Korean marinades got me thinking: Does that mean it works well with other Korean flavors like kimchi? It definitely does!

If you can find Asian pears, by all means, use them. Otherwise, this works great with fresh green apple, too.

1 lb (0.5 kg) Asian pears or Granny Smith apples

1 clove garlic, grated

1 tsp (6 g) ginger, grated

2 tbsp (30 ml) *gochujang*

1 tbsp (20 g) salt

1 tsp Asian fish sauce, omit for vegan, optional

Peel and core the apples. Slice into ¼-inch- (6-mm-) thick slices. Mix all of the ingredients together and be a little rough with the apples to release some of their juice.

Sanitize a glass jar and add the apples. Seal and keep in the fridge for a day. For the first couple of days, they will be crisp. But the longer you wait, the more they will infuse. Keep for up to 3 weeks.

PROJECT PARLOR
2012 SUMMER BBQ
COMPETITION
WINNER

WHIPPED SSAMJANG

Whenever I get a steaming bibimbap in a stone bowl, I press the rice against the scalding hot sides to crisp it up, and I add a ton of deep red *ssamjang*. It's umami-packed Korean hot sauce that I can't get enough of. My version is a cross between the traditional sauce and the creaminess of ranch dressing.

You can find *doenjang* and *gochujang* in Korean food aisles or specialty stores.

¼ cup (60 ml) fermented soybean paste, known as *doenjang*

1 tbsp (15 ml) *gochujang*

2 cloves garlic, grated

1 scallion, roughly chopped

1 tsp (5 ml) maple syrup or sugar

3 tsp (15 ml) sesame oil

¼ cup (60 ml) cream cheese

2 tbsp (30 ml) heavy cream

Blend all of the ingredients except the heavy cream with an immersion blender or food processor. Mix until the sauce is completely smooth, stop to scrape the sides of the bowl with a spatula. Transfer the sauce to a plastic container and stir in the heavy cream. Store in the fridge for up to two weeks.

BOTH
PROJECT PARLOR
2012 SUMMER BBQ
COMPETITION
WINNERS

SAVORY YOGURT

Throw out any ideas you have about yogurt and granola. Think of yogurt as a palette for everything, not just sweet dishes. I love this savory yogurt with poached egg and paprika on my Korean sub sandwich and as simple dip for salty, wavy potato chips.

1 pint (475 ml) plain yogurt

1 clove garlic, grated

1 tsp (6 g) salt

¼ cup (40 g) chives, finely chopped

1 tsp (6 g) white pepper

Half and half or heavy cream, optional

Whisk all of the ingredients together, except the heavy cream, in a medium bowl. Pour into a squeeze bottle, cover the top with plastic and screw on the top. Remove the plastic layer before using it.

If the chives are too big for the spout, cut the spout if you can. If not, store in a jar and use as a spread with a knife or spoon. If you want to thin it out more, add 2 tablespoons (30 ml) of half and half for an easy-to-squirt sauce or heavy cream for a rich, thicker consistency.

MEYER LEMON MAYO

MAKES: 1½ cups (355 ml) mayo
TOTAL TIME: 10 minutes

It is so satisfying to make your own condiments. Once I discovered the glory of emulsification, I never looked back. Please note: this recipe calls for zest of two lemons but the juice of only one, so wrap that other lemon for later or have a quick lemonade!

1 egg yolk

½ tsp salt

½ tsp Dijon mustard

½ tsp honey

2 Meyer lemons, both zested and 1 juiced

1 tbsp (15 ml) white champagne vinegar

1 cup (240 ml) vegetable oil

In a clean pint jar, place the egg yolk, salt, mustard, honey and lemon zest. Using an immersion blender, pulse the mixture twice to quickly incorporate. Add the lemon juice and vinegar, mix. Leaving the blender on, slowly add the oil in a slow stream until you have a fluffy thickness that can coat the back of a spoon without slipping off. If the emulsification breaks and it is still thin and liquidy, add a squeeze of lemon and chill the mixture in the freezer for 5 minutes. Attempt to blend again. Refrigerate until ready to use.

TOASTED SESAME LMAO

MAKES: 1½ cups (355 ml) mayo
TOTAL TIME: 5 minutes

Same method as the Meyer Lemon Mayo (above) but with a toasty, garlicky kick.

1 egg yolk

½ tsp salt

½ tsp dry mustard

½ tsp honey

1 clove garlic, microplaned

1 tbsp (15 ml) black vinegar

2 lemons, both zested and 1 juiced

¼ cup (60 ml) sesame oil

¾ cup (180 ml) vegetable oil

In a clean pint jar, place the egg yolk, salt, mustard, honey, garlic, black vinegar and lemon zest. Using an immersion blender, pulse the mixture twice to quickly incorporate. Add the lemon juice and mix. Leaving the blender on, slowly add the sesame oil first and then vegetable oil in a slow stream until you have a fluffy thickness that can coat the back of a spoon without slipping off. If the emulsification breaks and it is still thin and liquidy, add a squeeze of lemon and chill the mixture in the freezer for 5 minutes. Attempt to blend again. Refrigerate until ready to use.

PROJECT PARLOR 2012 SUMMER BBQ COMPETITION WINNER

ROMANTIC ROMESCO

MAKES: 3 cups (709 ml) romesco sauce
TOTAL TIME: 1 hour, 10 minutes

Jeff and I fell in love with an episode of Anthony Bourdain's *No Reservations*. In Spain, he was at a backyard BBQ where there were steaming bunches of fresh scallion in newspaper. They doused the stalks in a muted-red romesco sauce.

Not only does it taste great on scallions but also anywhere you'd use a ketchup, with less vinegar sting and a more toothsome texture from the almonds. Purists will insist on peeling the almonds, but I like the texture they provide.

---

4 ripe tomatoes

1 cup (150 g) whole roasted salted almonds

4 roasted jarred piquillo peppers

1 lemon, zested and juiced

⅓ cup (80 ml) vegetable broth

1 tsp (6 g) paprika

1 tsp (6 g) salt

¼ cup (60 ml) olive oil

If you don't have a smoker, skip this step and use a ½ teaspoon of liquid smoke at the end. (Gasp, I'm SORRY.) Cut a small *X* into the top of each tomato. Smoke the tomatoes over indirect heat for an hour and until they crack. Carefully transfer them to a bowl to cool. They will release a lot of juices.

Peel the tomatoes and mash them. Add the tomato, almonds and peppers to the bowl of a food processor. Pulse the mixture until there are not complete almond pieces left. Add the lemon, zest, broth, paprika and salt. Blend for 1 minute, scrape down the sides and turn back on. Slowly add the olive oil. Blend until you have a smooth sauce.

Store in a sealed jar for up to a week.

BLACK BEAN SPREAD

MAKES: 1½ cups (355 g) spread
TOTAL TIME: 5 minutes

If you have leftover Cinnamon Black Beans (page 117), this is great as a warm dip for tortilla chips or to spread on torta sandwiches. I also love it because it is purple.

---

1 cup (150 g) Cinnamon Black Beans (page 117), drained

½ cup (120 ml) cream cheese

2 tbsp (30 ml) heavy cream

Blend the cinnamon black beans with the cream cheese with an immersion blender or food processor. Thin it out with the heavy cream. Add more to make it thinner, if you wish.

MISO DRESSING

MAKES: 1 cup (240 ml) dressing
TOTAL TIME: 5 minutes

Cooking for a wide audience has taught me how to be flexible. Most of the time, I prepare salads undressed and have a variety of dressings available to appease different diets and allergies. This miso-based sauce is both vegan and gluten-free.

1 tbsp (15 ml) white miso

2 tbsp (30 ml) tahini

2 tbsp (30 ml) calamansi or yuzu juice

2 tbsp (30 ml) cold water

3–4 grinds coarse ground pepper

Whisk all of the ingredients together. Taste it by dipping a vegetable in it. Dilute with more water if it is too strong for your taste.

Dress a slaw or zucchini noodle salad before serving. If you toss greens in this dressing, it will reduce the volume of the salad by half. Just a warning!

NUOC MAM CHAM

MAKES: 1 pint (473 ml) thin dressing
TOTAL TIME: 8 hours, 5 minutes

A fishy Vietnamese dressing for Herb Slaw (page 118), marinating proteins or dipping fried egg rolls.

The benefit of Nuoc Mam Cham is that a little goes a long way and it lasts longer than most condiments.

2 bird's eye chili peppers

5 tbsp (74 ml) Asian fish sauce

1 cup (240 ml) water

4 tbsp (60 ml) rice vinegar

4 tbsp (60 ml) sugar

1 tbsp (10 g) garlic, sliced thinly

3 tbsp (74 ml) minced capers

Depending on your tolerance for spiciness, pierce the chilis with the end of a knife (if you're a wuss). Slice them and throw in the seeds if you like fire in your mouth. If you cannot find Asian fish sauce, mash up 4 anchovies. If you want to make this sauce vegan, use minced capers.

Combine all of the ingredients in a jar and let it sit on the counter overnight. Refrigerate for up to a month.

PROJECT PARLOR
2012 SUMMER BBQ
COMPETITION
WINNER

DANDELION PESTO

MAKES: 1 pint (80 g) pesto
TOTAL TIME: 10 minutes

When I was working at Home/Made, I learned that the dandelion garnish I used for cheese platters was entirely edible. I didn't enjoy my first bitter taste, but once Monica doused it in lemon, it was great. I had thought of dandelion only as a weed that creeped up between sidewalk cracks or abandoned lots. It's a hearty green that you can cook down, too.

1 bunch dandelion leaves

¼ lb (113 g) Parmesan cheese, roughly chopped

2 cloves garlic

1 tsp (6 g) salt

¼ cup (22 g) sunflower seeds, shelled

2 lemons, juiced and zested

1 cup (240 ml) olive oil + extra

Cut off the first inch (25 mm) of stems from the stalks. Roughly chop the leaves and add them to the bowl of a food processor. Pulse the greens with the cheese and garlic a couple times to break them up. Add the salt, sunflower seeds, lemon juice and zest to the mix and turn the processor on low. Slowly pour in the olive oil. Stop the machine if everything sticks to the sides. Scrape down the sides with a spatula and continue to blend, adding olive oil.

For a smoother pesto, soak the sunflower seeds in cold water for 4 hours and drain. Conversely, you can also fold the sunflower seeds in at the end for a more rustic feel.

To store, transfer the pesto to a plastic container. Tap the container on the counter to even out the spread and remove any air bubbles. Top off the pesto with a ¼ inch (6 mm) of olive oil before sealing and putting in the fridge.

SAUERKRAUT

MAKES: a quart (946 g)
sauerkraut

TOTAL TIME: 20 minutes
active, up to 10 days passive

There is a fascinating phrase, *cavoli riscaldati,* which is Italian for trying to revive a long finished love affair. In addition to being one of my favorite toppings for hot dogs, sauerkraut can actually have a full afterlife. You can cook it down to mellow out the flavor or chop it up even further to make a relish. Cabbage may wilt, but kraut can last for what seems like forever.

1 head cabbage, shredded

1½ tbsp (30 g) salt

1 green apple, grated

2 tsp (11 g) fennel seeds

Toss the cabbage with the salt and let stand at room temperature in a mixing bowl for 10 minutes. Move the cabbage around, squishing slightly with your hands. Add the apple and fennel seeds.

Transfer the cabbage to a clean crock, pour in any liquid that emerged from your squeezing session. Use a clean plate to weigh the cabbage down and to ensure it stays submerged. Cover the crock with a tea towel or cheesecloth, store in a cool place for 3 days. Check that the cabbage is soaked, if not, add water.

After 3 days, taste the kraut. If you like the way it tastes, transfer it to a clean jar and store in the fridge. You can ferment it for up to 10 days total. Make sure to skim any crap that floats to the top.

If you don't have a crock, a large jar will do.

TOMATO SALT

MAKES: **1 cup (150 g)**
finishing salt
TOTAL TIME: **5 minutes**
active, 1 to 2 days passive

When I was beginning my culinary journey, someone very dear to me gave me my first fine dining book, *On the Line*, by Eric Ripert. It was autographed! However, I didn't know that Le Bernadin served primarily seafood. I flipped through the pages in awe, still very new to even eating sea creatures. I was intimidated by how complex the recipes were. I got to the appendix, and the only recipe I could make with the ingredients on hand was tomato confit. I had to start somewhere, and perhaps if you are a novice cook, you too can at least start here.

Now this is a real tribute to Eric Ripert's traditional tomato confit. The word confit comes from the French *confire*, to preserve. I can't think of anything else that lasts longer than salt. This is a really easy and fun trick if you have the patience.

1 ripe tomato
1 cup (150 g) coarse salt

Remove the stem and blend the tomato in a food processor. Pour it into a quarter-sheet pan with the salt. Alternatively, you can pass tomato through a box grater. Stir to combine and let the pan sit out in direct sunlight for up to 8 hours until the mixture has dried completely.

Chip off the salt and store in an airtight container in the fridge. It technically should be shelf stable, but I don't want you to sue me.

For a quicker method, preheat the oven to 175°F (80°C). Dry the salt with the door cracked open for 2 hours or until it has completely dried.

Sweet & Savory Surrenders

For competitions, I would usually outsource the desserts to my more talented baker friends, Emily Hanhan or Lindsey Case-Hayes. I always struggled with last courses until I realized that they didn't have to be sweet. Cheese courses are a European tradition that hasn't carried over to modern American society, yet! Here is a collection of both sweet and savory ways I like to finish a meal.

LESSONS LEARNED

- Know your strengths and don't be afraid to ask for help.

- When something isn't working, scrap it and come back later.

- Dessert doesn't have to be sweet!

CHOCOLATE BARK

MAKES: 2½ cups (450 g) bark
TOTAL TIME: 3 hours,
15 minutes

I am a dessert idiot, and this is the easiest and most impressive looking dish I can turn out for a party. You can replace the mixture of fruit and nuts or add pretzels as long as it equals the same total volume listed. I like to cut the bark into jagged asymmetrical shapes; no two pieces are the same!

Olive oil

1 (20-oz [560-g]) bag white chocolate chips

1 (20-oz [560-g]) bag dark chocolate chips

2 tbsp (20 g) dried pears

2 tbsp (20 g) dried cherries

2 tbsp (20 g) dried apricots

¼ cup (40 g) toasted walnuts

1 tsp (6 g) fleur de sel

Oil a quarter-sheet pan with a paper towel. Start boiling water in the bottom half of a double boiler. Reduce the heat to a light simmer and place the white chocolate into the top pot of the double boiler. Stir every minute until the chocolate is smooth for 5 minutes.

Pour the white chocolate into the pan; don't worry if it doesn't settle evenly. Melt the dark chocolate in the double boiler, swirling in any leftover white chocolate. Once it is melted, fill in the rest of the pan. Tap the pan against the countertop a couple times to even out the chocolate. Take a toothpick, skewer or knife and make a couple swirls between the two chocolates. Tap the pan against the counter again.

Place the dried pears or larger fruits onto the chocolate first, then sprinkle the smaller fruits, nuts and finish with an even sprinkle of the salt. Refrigerate uncovered for an hour. Wrap it in plastic wrap and store for at least 2 hours to set.

(NOT SORRY) BERRY SHORTCAKE

MAKES: 8 to 10 shortcakes
TOTAL TIME: 20 minutes

Not only did I win a year's supply of bacon once in my life, I also won a year's supply of coffee creamer. It's a funny challenge because I don't drink coffee. I was pouring coffee creamer in everything from my tea to oatmeal and hot chocolate. Baking with it was the biggest discovery. It can take the place of heavy cream and some sugar in recipes.

These easy shortcakes house berries and a decadent concoction of marshmallow cream cheese.

---

2 cups (440 g) self-rising flour

1 cup (240 ml) flavored coffee creamer, plus 2 tbsp (30 ml) for brushing

8 oz (225 g) cream cheese

1 (7-oz [210-ml]) jar marshmallow fluff

2 cups (440 g) any berries, washed

Preheat the oven to 425°F (218°C).

Mix the self-rising flour and coffee creamer to form a sticky dough. Grease a 3 x 4–cup muffin pan and divide the dough evenly into the cups. Brush each cake with more creamer. Bake for 10 minutes and let cool.

Whip the cream cheese and the marshmallow until it forms a smooth spread. It will appear difficult at first, but have faith.

Slice strawberries into discs and leave blue, black and raspberries whole.

To serve, split a creamer cake, spread marshmallow cream cheese on the bottom half, sprinkle on berries and top with the remaining cake.

Don't apologize when you serve. You're not sorry for doing this.

THIIIICK APPLE PANCAKES

MAKES: **4 large pancakes**
TOTAL TIME: **20 minutes**

These pancakes have heft. They're so flavorful and packed with chunks of apple that you really don't need syrup (which I don't like putting on pancakes anyway!). All you need a cute pat of butter and you're set.

1 cup (150 g) all-purpose flour

2 tbsp (30 ml) granulated sugar

2 tsp (11 g) baking powder

⅔ cup (160 ml) RumChata, horchata or rice milk with a dash of cinnamon

⅓ cup (80 ml) caramel-flavored coffee creamer or heavy cream

½ tsp salt

1 egg

1 fuji apple, cubed

2 tbsp (30 ml) bacon fat, butter or vegetable oil

Whisk the dry ingredients in a mixing bowl. Add everything else but the apple and fat. Mix until the batter comes together. Fold in the apples.

For each pancake, melt a small spoonful of fat in a frying pan on medium-low heat. Pour ⅓ cup (80 ml) of batter into the pan and cook until bubbles form on its surface. Flip the pancake and cook for 2 to 4 minutes until both sides are golden brown. Store finished pancakes in a warm oven until ready to serve.

MY FAVORITE CHEESES

When I was interning at Murray's Cheese, I heard about the American Cheese Society (ACS). Every year cheesemakers enter their wheels, big and small, to be adjudicated by a panel of experts. The interesting thing is that the cheeses aren't competing against each other but are scored on a rubric of technical prowess and aesthetic. So there are many winners to be found at your local cheese shop!

Another notable event is the Cheesemonger's Invitational in Queens, New York City. Cheese shops from all over the country fly a representative to compete in feats of skill including cutting exactly ½ a pound (230 g) of cheese, wrapping quickly and presenting the best pairings. It's really fun to watch and eat a smorgasbord of cheeses.

Here's how I like to enjoy some of my favorite cheeses:

ON TOAST, WITH CHAMPAGNE OR BOTH!

Brilliat Savarin + berries

Burrata + pesto

Cremont + honey

Coupole, by the spoonful!

Hummingbird

La Tur

Up in Smoke

WITH BEER

Challerhocker

Berkswell

Hoch Ybrig

L'Etivaz

Pleasant Ridge Reserve

Tubby

DARK CHOCOLATE AND CHERRIES

Caveman Blue

Rogue River Blue

SPECIAL OCCASION

Greensward and walnuts

Harbison and prosciutto

Hudson Flower

VEGAN WHIPPED CHEESE

MAKES: a pint (947 g)
vegan cheese
TOTAL TIME: 4 hours,
35 minutes

One of my favorite cheese spreads is Alon Shaya's whipped feta, goat cheese and cream cheese that accompanies his whole roasted cauliflower recipe. It's a showstopper of a dish. But what about our nondairy friends? How can we recreate this experience for people who cannot digest this lovely thing? I looked to the versatility of cashew nuts. Once they are soaked, they blend into a sumptuous paste, ready for any flavors you have to provide.

½ cup (75 g) raw cashews

1 lemon, juiced and zest reserved

Salt to taste

1 cup (240 ml) dairy-free sour cream (such as Tofutti)

1 tsp (6 g) sumac

¼ cup (15 g) fresh mint

Soak the cashews in cold water for 4 hours. Drain the nuts and blend with the lemon juice, zest, a pinch of salt and sour cream in a food processor until smooth. Chill in the fridge for 30 minutes before serving. Finish with a sprinkle of sumac and garnish with fresh mint.

LABNEH

MAKES: 1½ cups (270 g) labneh
TOTAL TIME: 5 minutes active, 2 days passive

I was having dinner at Glasserie in Greenpoint, and the server warned me not to eat the cheesecloth that was wrapped around the labneh cheese I got with my side of grilled flatbread. In that moment, the idea of straining yogurt clicked in my head, and I researched how to do it. It is incredibly simple, and you can do this with all manner of yogurt flavors. Add chives for a bagel spread or use peach yogurt to make a dessert cheese for pound cake. I like to substitute sour cream with labneh on nachos for a more firm cream cheesy texture.

1 pint (475 ml) yogurt

Line a mesh strainer with cheesecloth, making sure the excess flows over the sides. Place the strainer in the mixing bowl. Spoon the yogurt over the cheese cloth and wrap the remaining cheesecloth over it. Strain at room temperature for an hour, cover the top with plastic wrap and move to the fridge.

Pour off and save the whey that drips out. After two days, you will have a spreadable cheese. Remove the cheesecloth and store in a sealed plastic container for up to a week.

Whey can be used to constitute broths, smoothies and to thin out sauces. It has a pale, cloudy white color but blends in almost effortlessly.

MOZZARELLA PURSES

MAKES: **6 purses**
TOTAL TIME: **10 minutes active, 1 day passive**

When I interned at Murray's Cheese shop, I also helped during their mozzarella-making classes. After every class, I got to take home my own hand-pulled ball! On a picnic trip to Governor's Island, I wanted to bring it, but I didn't want to mess around with knives or the brine. A little prep and twine saved the day.

1 ball fresh mozzarella

Pepper

6 leaves fresh basil

6 pieces prosciutto

Slice the cheese into 6 even pieces and lightly pepper them. Wrap a basil leaf around each piece and then wrap the prosciutto over it several times. Secure the purse tightly with twine, tie a knot.

Place the purses on a cooling rack nested in a baking sheet to catch the whey. Let them dry in the fridge overnight. Pat the purses dry and store them in a plastic container. Consume them within 2 hours, unrefrigerated.

GROWN-UP HANDI-SNACKS

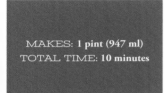

Stock up on buttery crackers and pretzel sticks for this update to a school-lunch favorite, Handi-Snacks. You can mix the types of cheddar in this recipe, but in my experience, the crappier the quality, the smoother it will be in the end. Artisanal cheeses will be too dry. I also love using Porkslap pale ale but any lighter beer will work. If you do not use stale beer, it will bubble and separate the cheese. It will also taste a little too much like beer. Luckily the soy sauce and mustard balance it right out. You can slather this on hot dogs, burgers or even add a cup (240 ml) of broth to make it a fondue.

1 lb (450 g) cheddar, cubed

1 clove garlic, grated

½ tsp ancho powder

2 tsp (10 ml) soy sauce

2 tsp (10 ml) Dijon mustard

1½ tsp (8 g) onion powder

¾ cup (180 ml) stale beer, opened the night before and left out on the counter

Put all of the ingredients except the beer in the bowl of a food processor. Pulse it until you've broken the cheese up into pellets. Add a little of the beer and turn the food processor on low. Continue to pour the beer until it is incorporated. Stop the machine and scrape down the sides. Turn the processor on high for 2 minutes, until the cheese is smooth. Store in a sealed plastic container for up to a week.

SHROPSHIRE BLUE QUESO FUNDIDO

MAKES: 1½ cups (270 g) queso
TOTAL TIME: 10 minutes

Do your nachos need a funky twist? Replace orange nacho cheese with a stinky blue cheese. Any blue cheese like Point Reyes, Gorgonzola or Bayley Hazen will work, but I like Shropshire because it is orange.

1 small cured chorizo, skin removed and roughly chopped

1 tsp (5 g) butter

1 tsp (6 g) flour

1 cup (240 ml) heavy cream

¼ lb (113 g) Shropshire blue cheese

Zest 1 lemon

4 warm flour tortillas

Tortilla chips

Shred the chorizo in a food processor, set aside.

Melt the butter on medium heat in a saucepan. Add the flour and cook for 1 minute until it forms a roux. Add the heavy cream and bring it to a simmer. Whisk to combine and crumble in the blue cheese.

Bring the heat down to low and continue stirring until the cheese melts completely. Take the pan off the heat, fold in the chorizo and garnish the fondue with lemon zest. If the cheese flavor is too intense for you, add some lemon juice. In the case that the sauce is too thick, whisk in more heavy cream.

To eat, roll up warm flour tortillas and dip them or serve with tortilla chips slightly warmed in the oven.

CHÈVRE BRÛLÉE

MAKES: 12 bites
TOTAL TIME: 20 minutes

During one of my grilled-cheese Sundays, I was trying to reimagine what I would serve. What if, instead of main course with melty cheese, it was dessert-like and kind of sweet? We had a salad that night, and everyone wondered where the grilled cheese was. I broke out my kitchen torch and served up these cute bites.

¼ cup (60 ml) superfine sugar

1 tsp (6 g) cinnamon

1 egg

⅛ cup (30 ml) milk

1 loaf of brioche, sliced into 1-inch (25-mm) pieces

1 (8-oz [230-g]) log goat cheese

1 cup (150 g) raspberries, halved

Preheat the broiler on low.

Whisk the sugar and cinnamon together. Divide the mixture in half and set 1 aside. Beat the egg with the milk and add half of the cinnamon sugar.

Cut the brioche slices into rounds by pressing a cup into them.

Dip 1 face of each brioche round in the egg mixture. Place dry side down on a baking sheet. Broil the bread for 3 to 4 minutes until the egg is no longer liquidy. You can also pan fry them in butter for 2 minutes on each side.

Roll the goat cheese into 12 evenly sized balls. Flatten them and shape like a peppermint patty. Dip 1 side of the goat cheese patty in the cinnamon sugar and place onto the top of a cooked brioche round.

Torch the cheese for 30 seconds on the baking sheet until the sugar bubbles and no longer looks like crystals. Alternatively you can stick these under the broiler for 2 minutes, too.

Top each brûlée with a raspberry half, cut-side down.

PANTRY ITEMS

I've scoured the markets in Brooklyn and Manhattan for these specialty ingredients. In the case you cannot locate something, I've listed replacements below. If all else fails, check Amazon.com.

Amarula—An African liqueur. Can be swapped out with RumChata, horchata or rice milk with a dash of vinegar and cinnamon.

Black vinegar—Chinese rice vinegar found in specialty aisles or markets. Replace with diluted balsamic.

Bonito—Known as Japanese *katsuobushi* or shaved fish flakes. Replace with crushed anchovy.

Chive flower—Stalks that have grown a bud. In Asian produce markets or some farmers markets in the spring. In the case of pickling, replace with scallions halved lengthwise.

Cotija—A Mexican white cheese. It can come precrumbled or in blocks, to be crumbled. Alternatives include queso fresco or even crumbled Parmesan.

Crema—A Mexican dairy product comprised of heavy cream and buttermilk. Different regions produce different tasting milks and proportions. Replace with sour cream or plain yogurt.

Doenjang—A brown Korean fermented bean paste. It can be used as a dipping condiment, but is mostly used in sauces. Replace with medium dark miso.

Freeze-dried banana—Space bananas! Trader Joe's carries them. They blend into a powder very easily. Do not confuse these with banana chips. Replace with powdered banana-milk drink mix.

Fried shallot/garlic—Available in large buckets at Asian supermarkets. I prefer to use the shallot more often; the garlic can sometimes be bitter and oily. Replace with crushed fried onions.

Gochujang—Red Korean fermented chili paste. It is vegetarian and is the base of kimchi flavors. Replace with a mix of Sriracha, ginger and garlic.

Hoja Santa—A Mexican heart-shaped leaf that is a cross between sassafras and mint. It typically comes dried and is stored in the spice aisle. Replace with a mix of dried oregano and mint.

Lumpia wrappers—Filipino eggroll sheets. Stored in the freezer aisle of Asian specialty stores. If you can't find them, large wonton or eggroll wrappers are also suitable.

Mustard seed—Brown and yellow varieties are available in bulk on Amazon.com. Do not substitute with dry mustard.

Panko—Light Japanese bread crumbs. You can substitute regular bread crumbs, just note the texture will be denser, like that of a mozzarella stick.

Peppers

Ancho—A smoked version of poblano. Sweet with medium heat. Found dried in the Latin foods aisle or powdered in the spice section.

Bird's eye—Small Thai. A little goes a long way. Available fresh.

Chili de arbol—Small Mexican hot pepper. Available dried.

Guajillo—Mild to medium dried pepper. Available dried.

Jalapeño—Most common pepper. Green, spicy and fresh.

Jamaica—Also known as Scotch Bonnet. Very hot and sweet. Available fresh.

Piquillo—Sweet taste and no heat. Available jarred.

Poblano—Fresh green pepper with medium heat. Usually stuffed due to its size.

Pink curing salt—Not to be confused with the Himalayan variety. Available online or ask a local butcher for some.

Puff pastry—Available in freezer aisles. Replace with tubes of crescent roll dough.

Ramen noodles—Available dried or fresh from Sun Noodle, Sunrise Mart or Japanese specialty stores.

Red curry—Potent Thai paste made of chilis, ginger and spices. My favorite brand is Maesri, which comes in small cans.

Sambal—A coarse Indonesian hot sauce. Usually contains fish or shrimp. Available jarred, in the Asian aisle.

Sausage casing—Comes dehydrated in salt. Available from butchers or online. Reconstitute with warm water for fifteen minutes and then rinse the interior like you would run water through a hose.

Sumac—Lemony Middle Eastern spice. It is a deep, dark red-brown and tastes great on yogurt. Available at Sahadi's.

White miso—Light Japanese fermented bean paste. Available in refrigerated aisles.

TOOLS AND TRAVEL KIT

SPECIAL EQUIPMENT

Some recipes require special tools. If you don't have them, don't fret. I will explain other options.

Baking sheet—I only own one full-size sheet and many quarter sheets. The smaller sheet pans are great for organizing your *mise en place* or your ingredient set up.

Blender—You can use a blender instead of a food processor for sauces, but do not fill to the top with hot liquids. The pressure will build and pop the top off, even if you are holding it. Blend hot liquids in small batches. Avoid blending stalky vegetables, meats or ginger. The strings will get stuck in the blade.

Cooling rack—Despite its name, you can use a crosswire rack to grill or bake. Generally, I like to use one when there is something that needs to be dried or drained in the oven, or when I'm cooking small cuts of meat that would usually slip through the grates of a regular grill.

Dutch oven—Heavy bottomed pot great for large batches of food and for deep frying.

Food processor—I have a five-cup (1 kg) processor. Adjust your workflow if yours is smaller. Use a mortar and pestle instead, or mince food finely on a cutting board with a gutter or lip to catch any drips.

Food safe spray bottle—For spritzing things. Honestly, if you don't have one, use a clean hand to flick liquid onto the food surface. Clean hands!

Grater—A box grater will yield the largest grade for potatoes and semisoft cheeses. A handheld grater with smaller holes is what I use for cheese, garlic and nutmeg.

Grill—If you do not have a grill, substitute a grill pan. I have a double-sided cast iron one that produces excellent grill marks. Make sure to turn on your oven vent or open a window when grilling indoors.

Ice cream scoop—I keep a one-ounce (28-ml) mini scoop around for meatballs, cookies or biscuit dough.

Immersion blender—I have a Braun hand blender. It has one speed and no attachments, and it fits perfectly into wide-mouthed mason jars, so you don't have to transfer the sauce between vessels.

Mandoline—A vegetable slicer, sometimes available with width settings. Always slice with your palm down and fingers up.

Metal spoon—Be careful not to use metal spoons when stirring hot things. Do not leave an uninsulated metal spoon in a hot pan or you will burn yourself. Use these for scooping, serving and stirring.

Microplane—The smallest grade of grater for garlic, nutmeg or truffles. Be sure to rinse these right away or the food crust is near impossible to scrub off.

Smoker—For grill smoking, soak wood chips overnight in cold water. Build a fire on one side of a grill and let the coals turn gray. Drain the wood chips and place a handful at a time to smoke foods resting on the cold side of the grill. For smoking guns and stand-alone smokers, follow manufacturer instructions. If you don't have any of these things, seriously, just use a dash of liquid smoke. I won't tell.

Spatula—Use a silicone baking spatula to scrape every last bit of sauce out of a container. You did all that work, use every last drop! Other spatulas you need are a regular metal frying kind and a fish spatula. The latter is long and thin for delicate materials.

Spice grinder—It may sound excessive to have a second coffee grinder dedicated to spices but hear me out. The spice powders you buy in the store have a shelf life. Many spices have essential oils in them that lose their potency once you grind them. Grinding fresh guarantees you'll pack a punch. Clean your spice grinder by pulsing a spoonful of bread crumbs (and using them!). If all else fails, invest in a mortar and pestle. It's more of a workout, but gets the job done.

Strainer—A colander will not cut it for straining soups or labneh. You need at least a pint- or quart-size strainer to catch all of the little floaties.

Thermometer—Cooking proteins to the directed time is not enough to confirm food safety and prevent food poisoning. My kitchen equipment might be calibrated differently than yours, so use a thermometer to make sure something is cooked through.

Twine—Sometimes you need to tie something. Another way to make your own twine is to take a piece of plastic wrap and roll it between your hands to make a small rope. Don't use plastic twine directly on food or in heat, wrap in a protective layer of plastic or parchment.

Whisk—Use a whisk to whip sauces or batters. If you don't have one, use a fork or a set of wooden chopsticks.

Wooden spoon—A trusty staple in my kitchen! Use these for sautéing and stirring. Use the blunt end to smash spices or jam it in the oven door to dry out foods.

GENERAL TRAVEL

When I began to compete regularly, I started to collect supplies in a plastic bin that I brought with me. It has everything I need to serve food or host a pop-up.

- Aprons
- Cardboard boats
- Cheese grater
- Chef knife
- Corkscrew
- Disposable gloves
- Fish spatula
- Forks
- Ladle for liquids
- Digital thermometer
- Dry bar towels

- Foil
- Microplane
- Napkins
- Parchment paper
- Paring knife
- Plastic wrap
- Serving spoons, metal (2)
- Spoons
- Tongs (2 sets), for meat and veggie cooking
- Wooden spoon
- Zester

PICNIC

- Blanket to sit on
- Bug spray
- Tarp, if it rained the night before

GRILLING

- Charcoal
- Chimney
- Junk mail or recycled paper to start the fire
- Lighter

STAYING ORGANIZED

I didn't get wise about documenting my recipes and ideas until four years ago. To compile this book I had to secure a handkerchief around my nose and mouth to look through dusty boxes of papers under my stairs. Needless to say, I've learned my lesson.

I have a combination of analog and digital solutions to this problem of staying organized. I have a small, cheap pocket notebook that I keep near me at all times. It's filled with notes and various shopping lists. I start from the back of the book because I'm left-handed (I know, quirky). When I finish a notebook, I file it away on a shelf. This notebook is crucial when I sit bolt-upright in the middle of the night and need to scribble an idea down. I have a problem going back to sleep if I don't write it down. What? You don't do that?

On my fridge is a running list of what's inside as well as priority ingredients to use sooner than later. Sometimes I'll write ideas on it because I know I'll look there when I'm rummaging for a snack.

Digitally, I started using an app called Scrivener to manage my "to cook" list, blogs and writing assignments. It has an offline mode that syncs to Dropbox so I can write on the New York City subway, where there is no cell service or wifi. If I need to collaborate or get feedback from people, I put production notes in a Google Document.

Every week, I have a Google Document template I use to develop, cook and photograph three to five recipes. If I don't get to a recipe, I'll move it to next week's doc. I'm a fan of checking things off a list, so on a particularly active cooking day, I'll print it and go wild with my pencil.

Here's an example of my weekly activity sheet:

RECIPE 1

Ingredients

Theoretical steps

RECIPE 2

RECIPE 3

SHOPPING LIST

Farmers Market

Brooklyn Kitchen

The Meat Hook

INVENTORY

Fridge

Freezer

Counter

Pantry

FOR NEXT WEEK

Instagram has quickly become a way to show people what I'm working on and also how I remember what a dish looked like. I've set up a fun digital contraption with If This Than That (IFTTT.com). Every time I publish a photo on Instagram, IFTTT sends a copy of the photo to my Google Drive with the caption. Now I can search my Google Drive for a dish if I'm going to write the recipe for it.

My workflow might not work for everyone, but I believe that everyone drinks a different social media cocktail. One of my favorite things to do is to scour the website ProductHunt.com for new apps to try. You might find something that works for you there.

MENUS AND PARTY IDEAS

I understand if you don't read this cookbook straight through (Gosh, who *does* that?!). A lot of my recipes fit together. Here are ideas to mix and match them. I'd love to hear about combinations you come up with!

MODERN KOREAN BBQ

Brooklyn Bulgogi (page 93)

Kimchi Apples (page 151)

Miso Curry Onigiri (page 99)

Whipped Ssamjang (page 152)

RAINY DAY

Lazy French Onion Soup (page 32)

Thiiiick Apple Pancakes (page 166)

GETTING OVER A COLD

Nanay's Arroz Caldo (page 39)

Geri Halliwell, You Know, Ginger Spice! Chili (page 20)

DIM SUM

Shumai, Oh My (page 71)

Chinese Sausage (page 55)

Miso Gritty (page 135)

Hen of the Woods Bouquets (page 130)

BURGER NIGHT

"I Like It Shallot" Burger (page 100)

Black Bean Burgers (page 105)

"Fries" (page 116)

Potato Salad with Wasabi Sesame Seeds (page 120)

OKTOBERFEST

Longaniza (page 58)

Sauerkraut (page 157)

Grown-Up Handi-Snacks (page 173)

FIESTA

Chicken Mole Torta (page 87)

Roasted Stuffed Poblano Flatbread (page 91)

Carne Asada (page 83)

Crunchy Elote (page 96)

Cher-Meow-la (page 151)

¡Watermelon! (page 124)

RUSTIC PICNIC

Chopped Chickpea Sandwich (page 123)

Grilled Stone Fruit (page 113)

Mozzarella Purses (page 172)

WINTER IS COMING

Whole Lemongrass Chicken (page 110)

The Smokemonster (page 29)

Herb Slaw (page 118)

TEA PARTY

Spiced Ham Butter (page 127)

(Not Sorry) Berry Shortcake (page 165)

Wonton Fruit Cup (page 133)

OTHER FUN THINGS TO TRY

Thiiiick Apple Pancakes (page 166) and broken up Chocolate Bark (page 162)

Labneh (page 171), Bacon Chili Oil (page 67) and grilled bread

Fatty Fat Tortillas (page 64), Pulled Chicken Mole (page 84) and Savory Yogurt (page 152)

Grown-Up Handi-Snacks (page 173) and Chorizo (page 56)

Black Bean Burgers (page 105) inside a Roasted Stuffed Poblano Flatbread (page 91)

Chopped Chickpea Sandwich (page 123) or Bitters Melon Salad (page 121) in a wonton cup

Kimchi Apples (page 151) and Herb Slaw (page 118)

Lob Gnarleys (page 136) and heavy cream makes a dip for Lumpia Chips (page 134)

Miso Curry Onigiri (page 99) coated with Chicken Dust (page 144)

Mustard Crème (page 149) and Bacon Tartine (page 75)

VEGAN RECIPES

Many recipes can be made vegetarian, but here is a quick list of what's already vegan.

Advieh Spice Mix (page 144)

Ancho Achuete Oil (page 145)

Chocolate Bark (page 162)

Chermoula (page 150)

Cinnamon Black Beans (page 117)

Lumpia Chips (page 134)

Miso Dressing (page 155)

Pickled Chive Buds (page 147)

Romantic Romesco (page 154)

Sauerkraut (page 157)

Tomato Salt (page 158)

Vegan Whipped Cheese (page 169)

Wild Mushrooms (page 178)

HOMEWORK

Studying on my own was the key to my cooking career. My hope is that in sharing my sources and self-assigned homework, you can take away as much as I have.

Bourdain, Anthony. *Kitchen Confidential: Adventures in the Culinary Underbelly.* **New York, NY: Bloomsbury, 2000. Print.**

What was meant as a cautionary tale of the culinary school and restaurant industry life fueled my fire and made me crave the camaraderie of chef life.

Buford, Bill. *Heat: An Amateur's Adventures as Kitchen Slave, Line Cook, Pasta Maker, and Apprentice to a Dante-quoting Butcher in Tuscany.* **New York: Alfred A. Knopf, 2006. Print.**

Career changes are okay no matter your age. Immerse yourself in it. Ask questions. Break down a whole pig in your small Manhattan apartment . . .

Besa, Amy, and Romy Dorotan. *Memories of Philippine Kitchens: Stories and Recipes from Far and Near.* **New York: Stewart, Tabori & Chang, 2006. Print.**

A lot of my recipes are remixes or updates to traditional Filipino foods.

Escoffier, A. *The Escoffier Cook Book: A Guide to the Fine Art of French Cuisine: The Classic by the Master Chef.* **New York: Crown, 1989. Print.**

I loved reading recipes in paragraph form. They helped me understand basic French cookery concepts like the mother sauces.

Hamilton, Gabrielle. *Blood, Bones, & Butter: The Inadvertent Education of a Reluctant Chef.* **New York: Random House, 2011. Print.**

Biography of famed Bourdain favorite and owner of Lower East Side staple, Prune. Lesson: you can have family, food and a writing career.

Jenkins, Steven. *Cheese Primer.* **New York: Workman, 1996. Print.**

I read this reference book cover to cover like it was a Jane Austen novel. It also serves as my visual checklist of European cheeses to try.

Page, Karen, and Andrew Dornenburg. *The Flavor Bible: The Essential Guide to Culinary Creativity, Based on the Wisdom of America's Most Imaginative Chefs.* **New York: Little, Brown, 2008. Print.**

When I would get stuck on how to spin a new recipe, I'd crack open this tome for ideas of what paired well with my ingredients.

Pépin, Jacques, Léon Perer, and Tom Hopkins. *Jacques Pepin New Complete Techniques.* **New York: Black Dog & Leventhal, 2012. Print.**

It was very helpful to have visuals for basic cooking techniques. Now I know a julienne from a brunoise.

Ruhlman, Michael, and Brian Polcyn. *Charcuterie: The Craft of Salting, Smoking, and Curing.* **New York: W.W. Norton, 2005. Print.**

If you want to learn how to cure and smoke your own meats, this is a huge resource for how it all works.

ACKNOWLEDGMENTS

I'd like to thank:

My brother Mark for experiencing terrible coffee drinks alongside my early experiences with cooking. And for teaching me that there is always room in your "dessert tummy."

Grandma Lita and Uncle Bernard for the Filipino food inspiration, especially for this quote: "Stew without spice is like looking without your eyes."

Jeff Stockton, I'm sorry I made you lift everything. I'm glad for all the time we spent together groaning, cooking, watching scary movies, reading fantasy novels and hanging out at your bars. Fort Kickass is one of the fondest, winningest and most formative times of my life. Thank you for being my #2.

Angela Workoff, my biggest cheerleader! Thank you for being down with my maniacal ideas and for helping me butcher large animals in Lancaster. You always find a way to bring me back down to earth (or laugh uncontrollably). Natch!

Dylan Garret, never forget sausage day or the day you finally rescued your records from storage. This is for you: Ladies, "He's from Miami."

Monica Byrne and Leisah Swenson took a chance on my inexperience. It is rare that a cook gets paid a decent wage and gains real experience in a supportive environment. Thank you for imprinting your design sense of "Height! Drama!" balanced with alacrity, taste and high production value.

Matt Timms and Megyn Florence for giving me the space and opportunity to repeatedly fail—but eventually shine.

The Page Street Publishing team for giving me a shot with this crazy idea. Cheers to you, especially Liz, for answering all of my questions. What a journey to spend with you all! We did it!

Recipe testers:

- Alayna Lim
- Alex Teplitzky
- Caitlin Carson
- Carol Benovic-Bradley
- Emily Corvi
- Rachel White
- Samantha Raddatz
- Tris Miller

Thanks to my dear friends and family for the advice, opportunities, help in pulling off events, heavy lifting, brainstorming power and for drinking very large mimosas with me:

- Andrew Tracy
- Beth Griffenhagen
- Brian X. Chen
- Brian Fong
- Calvin Pia
- Chandana Das
- Chris Klassen
- Chris Worrall
- Conner Garrison
- Emily Hanhan
- Eric Robinson
- Jake Elmets
- Jen Wanous
- Jonathan Visconti

- Justin Warner
- Lara Heintz
- Laura Dopp
- Lindsey Case-Hayes
- Liz Higgins
- Matt Kiser
- Mia Quagliarello
- Michael C. Stewart
- Project Parlor
- Ralph McGinnis
- Reid Bingham
- Ryan Darrenkamp
- Sam Johnston
- Sean Padden

- SF Keough
- Steven Valentino
- Tommy Siegel
- Tommy Werner
- Union Pool
- Vance Spicer
- Yan Yan

ABOUT THE AUTHOR

Jenn de la Vega is community manager at Flipboard, is editor-at-large of Put a Egg on It and runs *Randwiches*, an award-winning experimental food blog and catering service. Jenn loves talking about food situations, digital art and technology. She has appeared on *Guy's Grocery Games* on Food Network and *ChefShock* with Justin Warner.

The term *randwiches* or "random sandwiches" was coined by two employees at Etsy, who were some of Jenn's first clients. The whimsical nature of the unexpected and educational food experience is what Jenn is all about. Her mission is to go above and beyond to support the creative class and their communities. She wants to inspire you to cook for yourselves and others. Jenn wholeheartedly encourages you to believe you have the ability to do things yourself. She resides in Greenpoint, Brooklyn. If you see her at the farmers market, be sure to say hi!

INDEX